Barbara Hadley, mother of three children, was born on August 2, 1964, in Dallas Texas, to an alcoholic mother and father. At the age of two, Barbara was taken from her parents and placed in the foster care system. Barbara was bounced between foster home after foster home never long enough to build a connection or a sense of stability. At the age of five, she was placed in a home that upon arrival she knew was going to be bad news, so that's when the six years of horrendous abuse began. That same abuse would change the course of Barbara's life forever.

I would like to dedicate this book, Memoirs of a Lost Child, to my foster parents who saved me when I was 12, reunited me with my older sister, and introduced me to God. This book is also dedicated to my oldest child and inclusively my only daughter. She was the one who encouraged and empowered me to write this book. She also helped me fight through the memories that flooded back when I put the words down to paper. She was there when I went through depression and she dried my tears. I also want to dedicate this book to my publisher who believed in the story I had to tell.

Thank you truly from the bottom of my heart.

Barbara Hadley

Barbara Hadley

MEMOIRS OF A LOST CHILD

AUSTIN MACAULEY PUBLISHERS™

LONDON • CAMBRIDGE • NEW YORK • SHARJAH

Ordering Information
Quantity sales: Special discounts are available on quantity purchases by corporations, associations, and others. For details, contact the publisher at the address below.

Publisher's Cataloging-in-Publication data
Hadley, Barbara
Memoirs of a Lost Child

ISBN 9781647504724 (Paperback)
ISBN 9781647504731 (Hardback)
ISBN 9781647504748 (ePub e-book)

Library of Congress Control Number: 2022917756

www.austinmacauley.com/us

First Published 2023
Austin Macauley Publishers LLC
40 Wall Street, 33rd Floor, Suite 3302
New York, NY 10005
USA

mail-usa@austinmacauley.com
+1 (646) 5125767

I would like to acknowledge my children, my grandchildren, and all my friends and family for their encouragement.

This is how my nightmare begins. I can remember being four years old; it was a nice summer day. This lady came to me and told me she was my caseworker and that I had to go with her. I knew that I was going to a new foster home. So, the caseworker got my things. I had a box of new clothes and toys. I kept my Thumbelina doll with me; she was my best friend. So, we got in the car and went on a long drive and pulled to another house.

When I saw that house, I said, "I know I'm not staying here." This house was so raggedy and fallen down; I didn't want to stay here. But we went on and pulled up in the driveway. These kids were outside, playing. When they saw us pull up, they came running to the car. This girl came up to the car window and licked out her tongue at me.

The caseworker got me and my things out of the car and walked up to the door and knocked. An old lady came to the door with silver-and-white hair. It was long and it was in two ponytails. The caseworker dropped my stuff at the door and left. The foster mother called that girl that licked out her tongue at me to put my things away. That girl took my new clothes and put water all over them, and then she took my Thumbelina doll and broke her head off. I told my foster mother what she had done, and then the foster mother just slapped me for no reason and told me to hang the clothes over the chair in the kitchen and let them dry. Then she turned on the burners on the top stove. I was crying because my doll was broke. I put the rest of my things away.

She told me to come and eat, then I went in the kitchen and sat at the table. The kitchen ceiling was fallen in. While sitting at the table, she put a bowl in front of me; it was beans with fat, a lot of fat meat. I tasted it and I did not like it. I told my foster mother I did not like it. She said I could not leave the table till I ate it. I sat there till it started getting dark, and all of a sudden I heard a noise; something was making a noise behind the stove. I was so scared. Then suddenly it was on top of the stove, a rat. It ran behind the stove.

Then her dog, Chopper, came in the kitchen, but she made him come back in the living room with them, so I couldn't give him the fat meat, so I thought, *I'll throw behind the stove; the rats will eat it,* and that's what I did. And nobody knew, so I told my foster mother that I ate all my food. She came in, and the first thing she did was check the trash, then she said, "Okay, you can go in the other room and sit down with the other kids and watch TV."

My foster sister would sit by me and start pinching and kicking me. When it was time to go to bed, there was this couch that made into a bed. My foster sister and I slept on this bed in the living room. My brother, John, slept in the other room.

All night, Sandra kicked me and she told me I better not tell or she would beat me up. I was so scared. She kicked me until we fell asleep, and all of a sudden she started screaming, saying, "Momma, Barbara wet the bed." I was so scared; I did not know that I had wet the bed. My foster mother got me up and started beating me with the buckle of the belt, and the dog, Chopper, was biting me while she was whipping me. She made me run some water in the tub, and she started bathing me and slapping me and putting my head underwater and then bringing me up. She kept doing this till I couldn't breathe. She did it about three times. She made me get out the tub and run some more water in the tub and take my sheets off the bed and put them in the tub. "You will scrub them in the morning, now go to bed." I said, "What is happening to me? Why did my caseworker bring me here and leave me?"

When morning came, my foster mother got up and fixed us oatmeal. It was dry with no butter or sugar. I didn't like it, but I ate it anyway. She told Sandra and John to get dressed and that they could go outside and play. "Barbara, you will not go outside. You will scrub those pissy sheets out and hang them on the line, then I will comb your hair."

I said, "Yes, Ma'am." Then she showed me on a scrub board how to wash my clothes and hang them out. I had to jump to pull the line down because I was too little to reach it. I was crying the whole time and terrified. I could hear the other kids playing; I wanted to play too. When I would jump up and grab the clothes line and get the sheets hung up, that dumb dog would come and snatch the sheets down and run with it; my sister and brother would be laughing at me.

Mother came out there and told John to put Chopper in the house. "Barbara, you got ten minutes to get those sheets hung or you're going to get the beating of your life."

"Yes, Ma'am."

"Hurry up, girl, so I can comb your nappy head."

"Yes, Ma'am."

Well, I finally got the sheets hung, and Momma started combing my hair. She would just pull it from the root and my scalp would pop; it was very painful. I would cry and she would pop me in the head with the comb. She would use Royal Crown hair grease to grease my scalp. I remember having two braids in the front and two braids in the back.

When she got through, she let me go outside to play. There was a big tree in the front yard with a tire swing and basketball goal. I was so happy to finally be able to play with my sister and brother; they were around the side of the house. They had an old tire. They would stand the tire up and run and flip over the tire. It looked so fun.

When I came over there with them and asked if I could play with them, Sandra said, "We don't want to play with you. You are so ugly. What's wrong with your neck? It's flat like a pancake. I know, let's call her pancake neck." So they started calling me that, and I ran in the house and looked in the mirror and noticed my neck was different and I was ugly.

I asked my foster mother about my neck. She said, "Girl, go outside."

"But Sandra and John are calling me names."

"So go outside," she told me. She never whipped them; they never got in trouble.

My foster mother babysat these other kids; they were sister and brother, not foster children. I can remember their mother dropping them off. She was an Indian woman. She would always be drunk and my foster mother would always argue. She would drop those kids off and drive away real fast.

When we would play outside, Sandra was always the boss, and she would say, "We not playing with Barbara today." And sometimes they would play with me if Sandra said so.

My foster mother also took in borders. When you went out the backdoor, there were stairs on the side of the house and rooms up there, and she would rent them out because we stayed next door to a club name, 'The Chat and Chew.' Our neighbor was next door, then the club people would walk down the sidewalk in front of the house and they would be drunk, fallen down. The music was so loud; sometimes they would knock on our door in the middle of the night, asking for a room. My foster mother would get out of her bed and rent them a room.

When we got up in the morning, we would eat our oatmeal, and then we could go outside to play. We would sometimes play 'house' up under the stairs. That's when Sandra would be nice and let me play. I liked playing house. Sandra would ask Momma if we could play with some of old spoons and pots and pans. She'd say yes, and we would pretend we were neighbors, and if it had rained the day before, we would make mud pies like that was our food. Momma would let us play for a while, then she would tell us it was time to go and find cans. Sandra hated doing that, so she and John would make me climb in the dumpster outside the clubs and get all the beer cans out the dumpster. It was nasty, and we would be out there for hours, looking and digging for cans. When we came home, Momma would be happy because we would have two big trash bags full of beer cans. She would tell us to always smash the cans so we could get more in the bags, then we would put them on the side of the house till Mom took them to the recycle place.

John's friend and Sandra's friend, Jen, would be at the center as well. They all went to school together. This school ran from elementary through high school. Sandra's friend, Jean, was pretty too. She had a heart-shaped face with long black hair, and John's friend was mix with curly hair. They would be laughing and calling me names at the center. After a while, they would stop and play basketball, and Sandra would be talking to her friend. I would be in the corner, jumping rope. I liked going to the center. We also walked to school. It wasn't that far. We had to cross some railroad tracks. That was all right; we never ran into a train.

The worst part was just getting teased every day to school and from school. My teacher's name was Mrs. Jefferson, and her husband ran a funeral home called Jefferson Funeral Home. Mrs. Jefferson was my first-grade teacher. She was so nice. I had a hard time with my A-B-Cs. I didn't know all my letters, and the kids laughed at me; I was so dumb.

School was out for the day, and I had to walk home with my sister and brother and their friends, being teased all the way. I hated walking home and going to school with them.

When we got home, John and Sandra's friends would ask whether they could stay a while. Mom told them to get permission from their parents; they did. John would play basketball, and Sandra would play house sometimes. Our mother let us walk to store or she would let Sandra go over Jean's house. Momma made Sandra take me. When we got over there, Jean's mother was so nice to me, but she noticed Sandra being mean to me and also telling Jean to be mean to me. Jean's momma didn't like what Sandra was doing. Jean's mom asked her daughter why Sandra treats me like that. Jean told her mother that I wasn't Sandra's real sister; that I was a foster child.

When we got home, we played outside. Mother then called us inside for supper; we always had beans of some sort and cornbread. The next day was school. I hated going because the teasing would start and the kids would make fun of me. The beatings continued and my whole life was bad. I made bad grades, so when I bought my first grade-card home, Mother looked at it and slapped me across my face and beat me in the head with a high-heel shoe till I was bleeding, and she put my head underwater in the tub, then she told me I couldn't eat because I had to repeat the first grade.

So, summer began. I hated it because I was home all day doing a lot of chores and getting blamed for everything and getting picked on constantly. Mother would get us up early in the morning and have all us kids go look for cans. We would pull a little red wagon around town, digging in dumpsters for cans. This was all summer. When we got home, Mother told us to get the cans from the side of the house and put them in the car. "I'm going to drop them off and go grocery shopping. John, you are in charge. Don't y'all kids be bad."

I was so scared when Mother left because I knew they were going to start teasing me and beating me up and being real bad. I was shaking in my boots.

John went and got his friend, Ricky, and he told me and my sister we better not tell. So Sandra said, "If you don't let Jean come over and play, I'm telling."

John said, "All right, go get her." I didn't say anything. I was happy their friends were coming over. That way, I wouldn't get beat up and teased. I had my toys and was playing by myself. I heard John and Ricky tell Jean and Sandra to come in the house and come in the bedroom. They told me to go outside and let them know if Momma pulled up. They left the door open, and I came in to use the bathroom. I went past the door and I saw them on top of each other with their clothes off. I didn't know what they were doing, but I knew it was bad.

They then jumped up and started running in and out the front door, chasing each other when all of a sudden the glass fell out the front screen door and broke the front-door glass. Oh my god, I was so scared!!!

John and Sandra's friends ran home, and John told Sandra they were going to blame it on me. I said, "Please, don't say that. I didn't do that. You know that I didn't do that; you all did that." They told me to shut up and I better tell Momma that I did it or they would beat me up. I was terrified. I had so many butterflies in my stomach, I didn't know what to do. The fear that I had waiting for Momma to get home was unbearable. Knowing that you are innocent but nobody will believe you, so you get beat and beat.

Momma finally arrived home. She blew the horn for us to get the groceries out the backseat and trunk. Momma was starting to get out the car when John and Sandra ran to tell Momma I broke the screen-door glass. Momma asked John and Sandra how it happened. They told her I was running in and out the door, letting it slam behind me. The glass was up on the screen door and it broke it. That was a lie, but I was too scared to tell on John and Sandra, and even if I told the truth, she wouldn't believe me anyway, so I didn't say nothing.

She told me to get in the house, then she slapped me and broke a chair over my head. I was lying in the bed with a bandage around my head. The neighbor next door was an elderly couple. They saw me going outside, hanging the laundry with a bandage on my head, but they never asked me what happened. They just shook their heads and went back in the house. I kept wondering when is the caseworker coming back to check on me so I can be removed from this foster home.

We would go to my foster-mother church. The name of the church was Bethal Baptist Church. I liked going to that church. They would give out snacks and sometimes we ate dinner there; the best food ever, no beans, and it was within walking distance.

The summer was over and school started. I was back in the first grade. My teacher said that she and I were going to work hard that year; I would get it that year. I smiled when she said that, but she just didn't know what was going on at home. I was just trying to survive and stay alive.

One day, I was walking home from school with my brother and sister and noticed a car in the driveway. It was the social worker. When we came through the door, there was a boy standing there with the caseworker. She said, "Barbara, this is your brother." He looked like he was about nine or ten years old. I was shocked when she said that; my mouth was wide open. I couldn't believe what I was hearing.

He knew me and he called me Barbara Lynn and hugged me. The caseworker said that my brother was going to live there with me. I didn't want my brother there. I was trying to tell the caseworker why I didn't want my brother there, but my foster mother kept looking at me. The caseworker asked how I was doing, I said fine. "Well, aren't you happy that your brother will be living here with you?"

"I guess."

Then the caseworker went to the car and brought in my new clothes and Eugene's stuff. When I said thank you to the worker, my brother tried to say thank you also. That's when we noticed he stuttered.

The caseworker said, "He has gotten better, but he will need speech classes," and then she got in her car and drove away. I was glad in my heart that my brother was with me, but I also was sad because I knew what my brother was in for. John showed Eugene his room. They had bunk beds, and Eugene slept on top.

Soon as Eugene put his stuff away, they started making fun of his stuttering. I told Eugene not to pay any attention to them and stay with me all the time. So, we got away from Sandra and John and got to ourselves, and Eugene started telling me that we have other sisters and brothers and that I was the baby of our family. I told Eugene that I was getting beat by this foster mother all the time and they were making fun of my neck.

I asked Eugene why my neck was like that and he said, "Barbara Lynn, I don't know," but he said, "Don't worry, I will take care of you. I won't let nobody hurt you again." I saw in his eyes that he meant it. He went to the same school as Sandra and John went to. The first day walking to school, John asked Eugene a question just to get Eugene to talk so they could make fun of him.

I told Eugene, "Don't say anything," but my brother wouldn't listen, and he started trying to answer the question and they started laughing at him. I grabbed my brother's hand and we started walking by ourselves. Eugene was so mad that he told me he was going to fight him if he kept on teasing him and messing with me. I was glad I had my brother there. We were finally together forever.

When we got home, our foster mother made us do our chores and go look for cans to recycle.

Eugene asked me, "Is this what she has been having you doing?"

I said, "Yes, and she has been beating me," and Eugene said, "Don't worry, I will protect you."

I asked Eugene, "Where is our mother?"

He said, "Barbara Lynn, I don't know." I can remember how our foster mother would beat Eugene because he couldn't talk right, and the teacher would send notes home about Eugene fighting at school because kids were making fun of his stuttering. This went on and on.

One day, I remember it was on a Saturday. We didn't have to go to school. Our mother woke us up early for us to go pick up cans. The night before, she didn't feed me or Eugene, but she fed the other kids, and she would always tell us that our mother didn't want us.

"Nobody wants kids like you all. He can't talk, and your neck. I'm the only one that would take you all in. Be thankful, and you all go pick up cans. If you do good and find a lot of cans, I'll let you all go walk to the lake with your friends, so, John and Sandra, do good."

"Yes, Ma'am." Eugene and I were happy.

Also, John told my brother, "If you and Barbara find a lot of cans, you can go with us." But I was so hungry, I couldn't even think about picking up a can. I told my brother, Eugene, that I was hungry.

He said, "Okay, Barbara Lynn, I'm going to get you something to eat." So, we began digging for cans in this dumpster behind this club and restaurant. I got in the dumpster, looking for cans, and found a sandwich, and I showed Eugene what I found, and he knocked it out of my hand and said, "Don't eat that, it's nasty." I said it's wrapped up, it's clean.

He said, "No, my sister will not eat out the trashcan. I am going in this store to get you something to eat."

"Eugene, how are going to do that? You don't have any money."

"Just stay over there and wait till I come out the store." Well, I did what my big brother told me, and he came out the store with all kinds of candy, and he told me to eat it then so John and Sandra wouldn't know what he had done.

"I told you, Barbara Lynn, that I would take care of you." We ate the candy up and started digging again for cans.

We found a lot of cans. We had to smash them so we could get a lot in the bag. We were gone a long time. We finally caught up with Sandra and John. They had a lot of cans too. But we had more than they had. We loaded the bags into the red wagon and started for home. When Mother saw all those bags, she was pleased. Mother told us to put the bags around the side of the house, and we could go to the lake and play.

So, then we began to walk to the lake. I always stayed with my brother because I knew he would protect me. So, we got to the lake and we all started wading in the water, and then all of sudden something took a bite out of my foot. I started screaming; blood was everywhere. Eugene came running and looked at my foot, and the white part was showing, so we had to rush me home. I couldn't put my foot down; I was limping. My brother helped me get home. John and Sandra were mad because we had to go. When they got me home, they started yelling for Mother.

She said, "What on earth is going on?"

"Something bit Barbara on the foot." She looked at it and packed it with dirt and told me to go to bed. The next day, it was all right. I stayed from school a couple of days. I was happy about that because I hated school.

Time went on and I went back to school. The caseworker would bring our new clothes out to the house. She would ask if everything was okay, but everything wasn't okay. It was worse.

Eugene and I were getting more beatings. Eugene was acting out at school because the kids were teasing him about how he stuttered. The caseworker never asked us how we were doing by ourselves. She always acted like she was in a big hurry, plus our foster mother was standing there, staring us right in our faces, so of course we said yes and she went on.

One day, Eugene came home from school early. The teacher brought him home because he had been fighting and talking back to the teacher. The teacher told our foster mom that Eugene had an anger problem. We had just walked up when I heard the teacher tell our foster mother the problem.

I was so scared for my brother. I didn't know what to do because I knew he was going, ready to get the beating of his life. The teacher had left and our foster mother had told us to go get our homework done. She told Eugene to go and get the belt, but Eugene didn't move. I was watching from around the corner. My foster mother went and got the belt. The look on her face was pure evil. She was whipping Eugene, and Eugene would not cry because he had gotten used to the beatings. He had been in the home for a year. The foster mother was whipping Eugene, and she had hit herself with the belt and that mad her angry, so she grabbed the extension cord and hit Eugene, and Eugene grabbed it from her, and she stopped whipping him and started calling him names, saying he was dumb and that he couldn't talk and saying our mother didn't want me or him and he would never learn and that we would always be in foster care. She told Eugene to go to his room and stay there the rest of the day, and he would not have any dinner.

And then she said, "Barbara, if you give something, you will not eat."

"Yes, Ma'am." I didn't have to worry about John or Sandra giving Eugene anything because they didn't want us there anyway. I was so worried that my brother would die of starvation. The next morning, she said Eugene could eat a peanut-butter sandwich. "I'm getting ready to go grocery shopping."

"Mom, can we go outside to play?" She said yes and that John was in charge. John always let his friends come over and play. They didn't play with Eugene or me, so Eugene and I played together.

Eugene said, "Barbara Lynn, I'm getting us out of here." Eugene was about 14 years old.

I said, "Eugene, what do you mean?" John went off to play with his friends somewhere, and Sandra too. Eugene went to the vacant lot right next door to the house and got these big, tall boards and said he was building us a house right in our backyard. Well, he got the boards when John and Sandra came back.

They said, "Eugene, what are you doing?"

He said, "Building me and my sister a house; we are getting away from y'all. I'm tired of you and your mother beating us and mistreating us."

John said, "I'm going to tell Momma and she is going to beat the skin off of you."

Eugene said, "No, she isn't, because I'm getting us out of here." It wasn't long before Mother came home.

She said, "What in the world?" John ran up to the car and told her what Eugene said. She had Sandra and John get the groceries out the car and told me and Eugene to go in the house.

Eugene said, "No!!!" I was so scared; I didn't know what to do.

She said, "Barbara, get in the house."

I said, "Eugene, please come in the house."

She started beating Eugene, and Eugene pushed her against the wall and said, "No more beatings." She was scared to death, and when Eugene walked away, she picked up a chair and called his name, and he turned around and she hit him with it, and it cut his eye open.

Blood was everywhere, and she said, "Now leave," on that. I ran to my brother to help him.

She threw me a rag and said, "Clean that blood up. Eugene, go to your room, and you better not tell nobody."

The next morning, we all got up. It was a beautiful day. It was nice outside. Mother fixed us oatmeal for breakfast. She called for Eugene. His eye was swollen shut.

She said, "Eugene, come here." He was so scared when she came near him, he jumped. She said, "Boy, I'm not going to hit you." She also put on a pot of beans with that fat in it. She then took a piece of the fat meat and put it on Eugene's eye, and then she told John to go get some red clay dirt. When he came and brought her the red clay dirt, she took the dirt and packed Eugene's eye with it. She told him, after he ate, he could go outside.

Our mother told us, "If anybody asks you all what happened to Eugene's eye, tell them he fell on the edge of the coffee table, you hear? Eugene, that goes for you and your sister, okay?"

"Yes, Ma'am." I am eight years old now. I was still measuring myself by the screen door.

My foster mother called us in the house to tell us that her uncle had died and we were going to the funeral. I'd never been to a funeral, so we went to the funeral. Eugene's eye was healing, but it still was noticeable. We were sitting there at the funeral and it was time to view the body, and when my foster mother went to look, he sat up in the casket. Everybody ran out of the church. The preacher was the first one out the door. The funeral people laid him back down and told everybody to come back, that it was all right.

Well, the funeral took place, but all the kids stayed outside because we were scared to death. Then we went to Frederick, OK, to visit her family. Mother went in the house, and we stayed in the car. While sitting in the car, a man came up to the car and opened the door. He started telling Eugene that he knew us and then he asked me whether I knew my A-B-C. I started saying them and he gave me some money and told me and Eugene he would be back for us; we never saw him again. Mother came out the house and we left.

When we got home, Mother said we could go outside and play. The neighbor next door was outside and they asked Eugene what happened. He told them exactly what Momma told him to say, that he fell on the edge of the coffee table. They looked at Eugene and just shook their heads and went in the house. They knew what was happening but did nothing.

Eugene told me that he was going to run away and that he would come back to get me. John and Sandra were somewhere, playing. They didn't notice Eugene getting on the bike and leaving; he had been gone a while. Mother called us in for dinner and called for Eugene, but he didn't answer. She asked me whether I knew where he was.

I said, "No, ma'am."

She said, "Girl, if you are lying, I will beat the black off of you." When she said that, I broke loose and ran as fast as I could. She told John and Sandra to go after me. I was running for my life. I got all the way to Patterson Center and got trapped, nowhere to go. They brought me back, and she told me she called the caseworker and she would be there in a minute.

"Go get a washcloth and wash your face and change your clothes; I will deal with you later. If she asks you if you are being mistreated, you better lie."

"Yes, ma'am." The caseworker came out and asked me whether I knew where Eugene ran off to. I said no.

"He didn't say nothing to you about he was going to run away?"

"No, ma'am." My foster mother said she might know why Eugene ran away.

"Eugene has a problem with authority, being told what to do. I had put him on restriction for fighting the other children I have in the house. Eugene is always fighting with the other children." The caseworker asked me if I was happy there.

I looked at my foster mother and said, "Yes, I'm happy here." She told the caseworker I am doing good, "But she's having a little trouble with her time tables at school, but we are working on it, aren't we, Barbara?"

"Yes, Ma'am." When the caseworker left, my foster mother gave me a box of cracker jacks for not telling the caseworker what was going on.

Well, the beatings continued till one day she had beat me and put my head through the wall in the living room for breaking a plate. She beat me in the head with a high heel shoe. I told God I was dead now; blood was everywhere. I got cleaned up and went to bed with nothing to eat.

The next morning, I was dizzy and my head was pounding. She made me go to school. While in school, I was trying to write my time tables and my head started bleeding on my paper. The teacher saw it and asked what happened to me. She told the class to keep working on their work. She got some paper towels, put it on my head, and walked me to the nurse's office. They asked me what happened. I told them that I fell. They kept questioning me. They called the principal in and then they started talking to the principal, and the principal found out that I was in state's custody.

My teacher said, "Barbara, you are safe now. You can tell us the truth. Did your foster mother do this to you?"

I started crying and said yes. I told them, "Please don't tell her I told you all. She will kill me." They asked me how long this had been going on. I said, "Since day one when my caseworker brought me there and dropped me off." They checked me out and saw the bruises, and the principal called my caseworker. She came and looked at all my bruises, and she asked me how long this had been going on.

I said, "From the first day you dropped me off."

"You mean this has been going on for five years? Oh my god."

I said, "Please don't take me back there, she will surely kill me."

The caseworker said I didn't have to worry; I wasn't going back there. "We are going to get your things and take you out of there." We pulled up to the house. She told me to stay in the car. I did. She talked for a minute to my foster mother, then she got my things and we left.

I went to this other foster home. The lady's name was Mrs. Smith. She had a husband and a son. I was scared to death. I was really scared of the husband. He said hello and I hid behind the caseworker. She talked to me and said it was going to be okay, but I didn't believe her. I didn't want to stay, but I didn't have a choice. I went in the house with my caseworker. I kept holding onto her. The foster mother asked me whether I wanted to see my new room.

I said, "I guess." She took me in there and the caseworker asked me to stay in there while she talked to the foster parents real quick. She told the foster parents how I was abused and that I wouldn't get in water. The foster mother asked why. The caseworker told her how the foster mother would hold my head underwater.

"She was trying to drown her." They talked for a while, and then she came and told me bye and that she'd be checking on me this time regularly, and then she left.

The foster mother showed me to my room. I never had my own room before; it was beautiful. I had my own bed and dresser. She told me to unpack and also she helped me put my things away. She told me that dinner would be ready in a minute. She showed me around the house.

My foster brother came out of his room to say hello to me. He seemed nice, but I was still scared and I didn't trust nobody. I stayed in my room till she called me for dinner. She told me to wash my hands before I could eat. I never had to do that before.

I asked her why do I have to wash my hands before I eat, then she taught me about germs, "You don't want germs on you or your food, do you?" I guess not, so I washed and sat down to eat with my foster brother and father, then they bowed their heads and told me to bow my head, and then we prayed. The whole experience was new to me.

The food was very good and no beans or fat meat, what a treat. Well, after dinner, Mother did the dishes and I stayed right by her side because I wasn't used to a foster dad and I was scared. I asked my foster mother could I wash dishes. She told me she would show me how one day.

The dishes were done and Mom went in her room, and I just stood in the hallway, watching my brother watch TV.

He said I could come in his room and watch television, but Mom said I have to take a bath first.

I said I didn't want to take a bath. She said I would be all right; she would be right outside the door. She got my towels and underclothes and pajamas. I got in the tub and started bathing, and I wasn't so scared because she didn't come in the bathroom. She just stayed right outside the door.

When I came out the bathroom, she was right there; what a joy. Mom took me in my room and started telling me about always putting on my robe because I had a father and brother and I needed to respect them and they would respect me and have their robes on, and that she was going to buy me some training bras because I was turning into a young lady; I never heard that before. She said she and I were going shopping for girl stuff. I was really happy but angry inside and confused.

I watched TV till I had to go to bed, and I said goodnight to Mother, Brother, and Father.

My dad said, "Goodnight, baby, and I am happy you are here." I didn't know what to think or feel about that, so I just went to my room and got in my own bed. I was in heaven, my own room.

The next morning, I was awakened by an awesome smell coming from the kitchen. It was Mom in there, cooking a big breakfast. We had scrambled eggs, sausage, biscuits, grits, pork chops, gravy; you name it, we had it. Mother told me to wash up and come and eat. I was shocked when I saw all that food.

I noticed it was still dark outside, so I asked my mother, "Why are we eating so early?"

She said, "Because your father has to get ready for work."

I asked him, "Can I call you dad?" and he said he would like that because he wanted to call me his daughter.

I saw that my mother was fixing his lunch for work. He had a gray lunch pail. I asked him where he worked. He told me he worked on a military base called Fort Sill.

Mother told, "Barbara, your father has to go to work, and you need to finish your breakfast before it gets cold."

I said, "Yes, Ma'am." Well, I finished my breakfast, then I went to brush my teeth and make my bed. Mom showed me how to make my bed and keep my room clean. She told me she was going to teach me how to wash dishes because that was going to be one of my chores. I finished the kitchen, and she told me to get dressed, that she was enrolling me in school today.

When I was getting dressed, I started thinking about my brother, Eugene, wondering where he was and was he all right. My foster parents were nice, but I was still longing and discontent and angry. I vowed that nobody would ever beat me again. I kept thinking about my brother, *I need to find my brother but where would I look?*

My foster mother dressed me real nice, and she told me I was going to get my hair done. She said that she had a friend that did hair and that she was coming to the house to press and curl my hair. I said okay.

I got enrolled in school. The school told me where to catch the bus at. The next morning, I got ready for school. I ate breakfast and my foster brother walked me to the bus stop. There were a lot of kids there. The neighbor's daughter that lived across the street was there. We were in the same grade, so she started talking to me at the bus stop. We had the same classes, so we became friends. I would go over to her house when my chores were done and we would study and play together. Her mother and my mother were good friends.

We also had a neighbor that lived next door to us who was real old, and she had a lot of cats, and her house was stinking and dirty, but she was a nice lady, and Momma always helped her. She had me meet Mrs. Brown. I was ready to go because the smell was so bad and I didn't like all those cats. Mom said I could be a big help to her if I volunteered to clean her house for her.

"After all, she has welcomed you with opened arms."

I said, "Okay, I'll ask her one day if I can come and clean her house for her."

Then Mother told me to get ready because her friend, who was a beautician, was coming over to do my hair. Mrs. Mable came and she was a very nice woman. I was so scared of her doing my hair, especially using a pressing comb, because my other foster mother used to hit me in the head and burn my ear and neck with the hot comb. I was very tender-headed; she tried to be gentle.

When she began parting my hair, she noticed all these scars in my head and asked me where I got those from. I told her my other foster mother. She called my mother in there and had her look at all these scars in my head.

She asked me, "Is that what your old foster mother did?"

I said, "Yes, Ma'am."

The beautician started pressing my hair. I held my ear down the whole time. She said, "Baby, you don't have to hold your ear down. I'm nowhere near your ear." I held it down anyway.

My hair was done; I really liked it, and she never burned me.

My foster dad came in from work and he hugged me, and I asked him could I have his lunch that he didn't eat. He said yes, so every day he went to work, he would save me his lunch if he hadn't eaten it. I couldn't wait for him to get home to see what he had saved me.

I started washing dishes every day for chores, and I didn't like it too much because I wanted to go outside to play with my friend across the street, but Mom said my chores and homework came first before any playing.

I was either in the fifth grade or sixth grade. I knew at school we were doing multiplication in math, and it was hard. My mother would always help, and I was starting to get the hang of it.

My foster dad would help me too, but I would get angry and say that, "I'm never going to get this; I'm just dumb," and he would say, "Don't say that, and don't give up so easy." I got mad and ran to my room.

I started thinking about my brother, Eugene, wanting to find him, and my family, my foster parents, did all they could to make me happy, but there was a void in my life; I wanted to know where I came from.

I was so angry at my brother, Eugene, for leaving me at that foster home to be beat. He said he was coming back to get me. *Why did he lie to me, or maybe he's dead?*

My birthday was coming up, and my foster mother was going all out of her way to make it the best birthday I ever had. She had her friend, Mrs. Wallace, come over with her daughter, Lisa. Lisa was way older than me, but she was very nice to me. We would sit in my room and talk about boys. I started telling her I wanted to join the basketball team at my school. "I'm scared to ask because I haven't been doing good in school. I'm so angry, because all my life people have been saying no to me and I'm tired of it. So, if I don't get to play, I won't talk to them anymore."

Lisa told me that my foster parents loved me very much. "I've known them for years, and they are good parents. Give them a chance." Lisa understood where I was coming from, because she told me she was adopted. I said no way. She and I visited for a while, and then they got ready to go. I really enjoyed talking to Lisa. After they were gone, I went and asked my mother about what Lisa had told me, and Mother said it was true. Lisa was adopted; they had adopted Lisa when they were overseas. Mr. Reynolds was stationed over in Germany, and that's where Lisa was from. They got her at six months old and brought her back to the States with them.

I saw a lot of Lisa because our mothers went to the same church. My dad didn't go to church; he didn't believe in giving all his money to the preacher. But both our dads worked on the base together.

Since she was older, she didn't hang around with me. She was into boys and hanging with her friends her own age.

Well, my birthday was here, I turned 10 and Mom baked me a cake and I had some friends come over, and for my birthday I got a record player and perfume. When I saw what I got, I was happy but also said that day I couldn't stop thinking about my brother, so Mom asked me what was wrong.

I screamed, "Nothing," and ran to my room.

Mother said, "Barbara, I have done everything to make you feel part of the family. What am I doing wrong, and why are you so angry?" She gave me a big hug and the party went on. Lisa and I went to the music store and I bought some records. I started playing my records and I enjoyed playing my record player.

One day, when Mother was cooking, I came to her and asked if I could join the basketball team at school; I really wanted to play basketball. Mother said she would talk it over with my dad.

I said, "Oh no, Dad is going to say no because of my grades. Momma, please, please, talk Daddy into letting me play."

"Barbara, I don't know. I will try, no promises. Now go and start on your homework."

"Yes, Ma'am." So, I got started on my timetables, and Mom helped me. I started getting better with my timetables and that made me and my mom so happy.

Dad came home and I gave him a big hug and he gave me his lunch, and then he and Mom went to the bedroom and shut the door and were talking. I knew Mom was talking to him about me joining the basketball team. I was finished with my homework, so I started cleaning my room and picking out my school clothes for tomorrow, then my dad called me to the room and said, "I hear you want to join the basketball team at your school?"

"Yes, sir."

"Barbara, I don't know, because your grades have been poor."

"I know. I'm trying really hard."

Mom said, "Yes, she is doing a lot better with timetables and her other work."

"I believe you are. I tell you what, I'm going to let you join, but if your grades don't improve, by your next grade card, I'm taking you off the team, so don't let me down."

"Yes, sir," I said and I hugged him.

Mom said, "All right, time to wash up and eat dinner."

Everybody got through eating. Mom and Dad went to their room, and I did the dishes. My brother was never at home, so when I got through washing dishes, I went and watched TV in the den. I watched all my shows till it was time to take my bath at 8:30 and be in the bed at 10:00 p.m. on a school night. Weekends, I could stay up till 12:00 midnight.

Well, I watched my shows, took a bath, and went to my room. While in the bed, I couldn't go to sleep. I lay there, thinking about my brother and finding my family, *Where are my real mom and dad? Why was I taken from them? What happened that I was placed in states' custody, and why did my parents give me away?* I would lay in the bed, thinking about all this, and then I would start to cry and get angry all over again. I would also think about the foster parent that beat me and all those ugly words she said to me, her and her kids. I was still scared to show my neck, so I would wear shirts with collars.

I finally fell asleep but was awakened by the smell of biscuits and sausage. This was every morning. Mom would cook a big breakfast. I really enjoyed her cooking.

My dad would be reading the newspaper, getting ready to go to work, and I would be getting ready for school. The routine at my house was go to school, do chores and homework after school; Saturday morning wash day, and Sunday church.

Mother told me breakfast was ready. I sat down to the table and Dad told me he was coming to my school today to pay for my basketball jersey. I was so happy that I didn't know what to do. I ran and kissed him and said, "Thank you, Dad. Oh boy, I'm going to tell all my friends that I'm going to play basketball."

Well, I started playing and enjoying myself. We would practice after school every day, and when I got home, I had to do my homework. I was so tired from practice, I would be doing my homework at the dining table and falling asleep. Mother would wake me and tell me to eat, shower, and go to bed. I told her I would finish my homework before class. She said all right and told me I had to start having my homework done so she could see it and do my chores. She said she was not going to be doing my chores for me anymore because I told them I would be able to play basketball and do my homework and keep up with my chores.

"Yes, Mother, I will be able to do my homework and chores." Then I kissed Mother goodnight and went to bed.

Another year had passed, Mother told me I had another beauty shop appointment Friday and my birthday was Saturday, and then we were having our first game Monday. I was so excited because we were good.

It seemed like my teachers didn't want me playing basketball because they would give me so much homework; I thought I would never get done.

I was so busy Friday, getting ready for my birthday party and doing homework. I got a lot of it done, so I decided to do the rest Sunday after church.

The next morning was my birthday. Mother fixed me a big breakfast, but something was wrong. I felt sad and angry all at the same time. Mother asked me what was wrong. I said, nothing.

She said, "Okay, come on and eat your breakfast and then start getting ready for your party."

"Yes, Ma'am." I finished my breakfast, did the dishes, and started getting ready for my party. Clothes were new, and my hair was beautiful. Mother and Dad also told me how beautiful I looked, but I didn't feel beautiful.

My friends started showing up, and we started playing games. I started complaining and doing a lot of arguing with my friends. I wasn't having a good time at all. I didn't know how to receive all this love and attention, and I also made a vow that I wouldn't get close to anyone.

My foster mother took me in my room and asked me what was wrong and why was I acting like that. I asked my mother why they were being so nice to me; I wasn't their real child.

I came out the room, looked at everybody, and knocked over my cake and ran outside. Momma told everybody to leave, that the party was over and to take all their gifts back. Mother was so angry with me when I came back in the house. She told me that I was going to clean up that mess.

She was very angry, so she just went in her room and waited for Dad to come home.

I cleaned up the mess and then I went to my room and stayed there. I began to wonder what was wrong with me, why couldn't I be happy and content, and what was going to happen when Dad got home.

I heard the car when it pulled up in the driveway. It was Dad. I didn't come out to greet him, but Mom came out the room and Dad noticed she had been crying, so he asked what was wrong and where was his birthday girl. "I got her something."

Mom took Dad in the room and they stayed in there with the door shut for a while. When they came out, they knocked on my door and said they wanted to talk to me in the kitchen.

My father said, "We have done everything to make you feel loved and welcome, but you keep turning us away. You let your anger get the best of you, and the people that are trying to get to know you and love you are the ones that you hurt."

"So, what are you saying, that you don't want me anymore and you're giving up like everybody else?"

"Barbara, we feel we have done all we could do for you, so we're going to have to let you go. So, tomorrow, I'm calling the caseworker and telling her to come pick you up."

"I'm so sorry." I ran to my room and slammed the door. I was full of rage. I said, "No, I'm not letting them put me in another foster home. I got to get out of here and find my real family and find my brother."

I started packing my suitcase. When I got done, I put it outside on the side of the house and crept back in the house.

It was about 7:00 p.m. when I knocked on my parents' door and asked if I could go outside and play with the neighbor's daughter across the street and so I can tell her bye.

They said, "Okay, but be home at 8:15."

I said, "Yes, Ma'am." I played with my friends awhile until their mother called them in, and then when they went in, I grabbed my suitcase and ran away. When my foster parents noticed that I hadn't come in from across the street, they came over and knocked on the neighbor's door and asked was I there. They told my foster mother I left about 30 minutes ago. She said that she thought I went straight home.

My foster parents looked for me but couldn't find me, so they called the caseworker. The caseworker came out and talked to my parents, and she just stayed there just in case I showed up. I didn't know where I was going; I was just walking and thinking about my brother, where would I look for him, and also thinking about how I have hurt my foster parents by running away; they must be very worried. Then I said to myself, "They don't love me. They're giving me up in the morning anyway."

Then as I was walking, it started lightning. I started getting scared because it was really lightning, so I started for home. I was hungry too.

When I saw the house, I noticed a car in the driveway, and when I knocked on the door and Dad came to the door, he had a mad look on his face. The caseworker was there and asked me where was I and did I know how worried everybody was.

Then she said, "Barbara, go get your things, you are going with me. Why are you acting like this? These are good foster parents. We don't have another foster home to put you in." I gathered my things, and my foster parents hugged me and told me they were sorry they had to let me go, and my mother started crying.

The caseworker told me to get in the car while she talked to my foster parents. When the caseworker got in the car, I asked her where we were going. She told me to a shelter until they could find me another foster home that would take me.

"Barbara, you have to stop being so angry and acting bad, because no family is going to take you."

I said, "I don't want to go to another foster home. I want to find my real family."

She said, "That is impossible; we don't know where your real family is, Barbara." My caseworker told me that she will try and find out as much information about my family as she could. In the meantime, she wanted me to be on my best behavior. "Can you do that for me, Barbara?"

"Yes, ma'am." Then she left. The people that worked there took my things in this room and told me to go in the recreation room with the other kids. I sat there, thinking, *What will come of me now?*

It started getting late and the houseparent showed me where my room was. I was so tired, I fell right to sleep.

The next morning, the houseparent told me that my caseworker wanted to see me. I came to her office and I was so surprised that she was beautiful. She was light-skinned with long, beautiful hair. She told me her name was Mrs. Banks and she would be my caseworker while I was in the shelter. She asked me about myself and we talked about the foster home that abused me. She was so nice to me, it seemed like we had a connection with each other. She really understood where I was coming from.

I looked forward to her coming into the shelter. Every day, we would get up and have breakfast. I started getting to know the other kids there. We would play games and watch TV, and, at 12:00, we would eat our lunch, and dinner was at 5:00. The food was all right, but that didn't matter to me.

The thing that did matter was me seeing Mrs. Banks come in to work. I was so happy that I found someone that I could talk to about what I was feeling, and she kept me from being angry, and believe it or not, I started being happy and content there. I hated the weekends because Mrs. Banks would be off. I thought I was going to die not seeing her for the whole weekend, but eventually I got through it.

One day, Mrs. Banks called me to her office and told me someone was there to see me. I asked who, and that's when this woman and man came out, and Mrs. Banks told me they were my new foster parents. They had come to take me home with them, and I said, "No, I'm not going nowhere. I'm staying here." And then I ran to my room.

The foster parents left and I never saw them again. Mrs. Banks came and knocked on my door to tell me they were gone and to come back to her office so we could talk. I came back to her office and she asked me why did I act like that, they were nice people.

I said, "They all seem nice in the beginning, but they change. I'm tired of going to foster home to foster home. Can't I just come and stay with you? I won't be any problem."

She said, "Baby, you can't stay with me. I work here. It's against policy."

I started crying and I asked my worker, "Will I ever get out of here?"

She said, "Barbara, your time is up here. We can only house kids here for three months. That's why I was trying to find you a home, so now I have to call your state worker and tell her that you refuse to go and that she has to come and pick you up."

"No, I don't want to go. You are my friend. You are the only person that loves me. Please don't do this, I will be lost forever." Well, she ended up calling my worker, and my worker told her to have me pack my things, she was on her way. I did as I was told. At this time, I'm 11 years old.

The caseworker came and took me to this girls' home in Taft, Okla. The town was so little, the only thing big in the town was the girls' home. We came to the office and this lady came out, spoke, and then she checked me in.

The caseworker and she spoke awhile, and then the caseworker came to me and said, "Barbara, this is your last chance. Don't mess it up. There's no other place to put you, so please be on your best behavior." I said I will, and then she left. I thought to myself, *An 11-year-old child that nobody wants and nobody loves.* I felt all alone and scared, but I didn't let anybody know how scared I was. I was tough and nobody was going to mess with me.

The lady at the front desk called over to the building next door for somebody to come and show me where I would be staying, so when this black lady walked through the door, she said hello and I was coming with her, that she was my houseparent. I asked what a houseparent was.

She said, "It's a person that runs the house for the girls. They are in charge of the house and girls." When we came through the door, I was shocked to see all these girls of different ages and color. They said hello and went on back to watching TV and shooting pool.

The houseparent called this girl name Charlotte and told her I was her new roommate and for her to show me where to put my things; she was very nice. The houseparent showed me around and told me the rules of the house and when laundry day was. I said to myself, "This is not that bad; I think I'm going to like it here." She also talked about how I get my mail, and if I needed anything, that was what the houseparent was for.

So, I finished putting my things away and I noticed that we all had numbers on our doors. I liked that; I could remember where my room was. After I put my things away, my roommate showed me where the TV was, and this room had a pool table. She said they called it the day room and that's where everybody would gather in the day room.

I asked my roommate, "Can we go through this swinging door here?"

She said, "No, it stays locked. The houseparents and important people can only be back there."

I said, "Oh."

She said, "Now on laundry day, they will hand out the laundry through those doors. Always on Friday, they will announce that laundry is here and everybody will line up and they will hand it out. That is why we have to put our names and room number on our bags."

Our rooms had two twin beds and two dressers and a vanity with a mirror in it. It was usually comfortable. Me and my roommate sat and talked, and then we went outside and she showed me that over to my right was the boys' dorm.

I said, "They have boys here."

She said, "Yes, silly." We started laughing, and it felt so good to laugh, and at that moment I knew I was going to be all right, plus now I had a friend.

We came back into the day room and nobody was in it. Everybody was in their rooms. She noticed me looking at the pool table and then she asked me whether I knew how to play. I said no.

She said, "Come on, I will teach you." Well, after losing a couple of games, I finally got the hang of it, and it was so much fun. I loved playing this game they called pool. I could play all day long.

"Breakfast is at 7 a.m.," she told. "The houseparents will announce it over the loudspeaker." My roommate told me that the building she showed me straight ahead and to my left was the dining hall. "You stand in a line and you tell them what you want and they dish it up on your tray." I sat with my roommate.

The other girls in the dorm starting saying hi and welcomed me to the dorm. I felt like they wanted to be my friends. I felt so warm inside. I felt like I belonged somewhere.

After we finished eating and walking back to the dorm, I saw the boys and I asked my roommate if we could talk to them. She said, "No, but we all go to church on Sundays, and we talk to them then, but we have to be careful that you don't get caught by the houseparent. Their houseparent is a man; the boys have men houseparents and girls women houseparents. So don't worry, we can go to church this Sunday. It starts at 11 and it is held at the gym."

"So where is the gym?"

"It's next to the cafeteria over there."

"Do you believe in GOD and go to church?"

"Yeah, to talk to boys; I'll be there. Oh yeah, I forgot to tell you that sometimes the houseparent will take us into town so we can go shopping or to the movies. We have vans that belong to the state that take us. We have to go to Muskogee because that is the nearest town."

It was already time for shifts to change. That's when another houseparent would come on. Their shifts were 3-11, 11-7, 7-3.

There was this one houseparent that I really liked. She was so nice to us girls. When she found out that I was new, she started talking and helping me and telling me how to stay out of trouble, like which girls to hang around and which ones to stay clear of, the ones that were always in trouble. Mrs. P was special. I saw that she cared about us girls. Some of the girls called her Mother P because she was the closest thing to a mother that some of these girls had. I asked some of the girls why was she so nice.

"She isn't nice for no reason. People are not nice for no reason. They want something." They told me I was wrong about Momma P. She really cared about the girls and that I needed to give her a chance. "I don't think so. I don't need anybody but myself."

I went to my room and started thinking about finding my sis and brother, and then the tears would begin to flow because I just knew it would never happen and they were probably dead anyway. I wouldn't never let my roommate see me cry because that's a sign of weakness and people see that they will run over you and take advantage. I vowed that I wouldn't let no one ever hurt me again. *I don't need any body because grownups are people that hurt children and lie to them. They will build up your trust and then let you down. That's the way I see it.*

So, every day, I would wake up and do what the houseparent told me to do because I knew this was my last chance. I enjoyed the place I was in. I would play pool, watch TV; I even started talking to the other girls. I came to this conclusion that this was going to be my home for a while, so I better make the best of it.

My birthday came around that summer, and I turned 12 years old. The girls that lived at the home all got together and bought me a chocolate cake, my favorite, and they bought me a present. I knew my best friend and roommate were behind all this, and I appreciate her for it.

The shift changed and it was time for Momma P to come and everybody was so excited. When Momma P came on, we all ran to hug her. Momma P had planned this party for me, and she bought me a present when she wasn't supposed to. She put her job on the line for me. Nobody had ever done that for me. I couldn't believe it. For me? I hugged Momma P so hard; I didn't want to let go. The party was great, and I realize that this was my family.

The Girls Home allowed different churches to come and preach and sing to us on Sundays. I never would go because I guess you can say that I was mad at God, because how could a loving God let me go through what I went through? I prayed for years for the beatings to stop, but they never did. They got worse and God took my brother from me, the only somebody that loved me.

Sunday came and my roommate asked me to go to church with her at 6:30 p.m. that Sunday evening, because this church which was coming was supposed to be real good. I told her that I would think about it, and she said, "Come on, Barbara. It's better than staying in the dorm, and your boyfriend will be there. You can see him."

I said, "All right." So after we ate dinner at 5:00 and came back to the dorm, we started getting ready. I was kind of nervous, but I started thinking about when I was at the foster home. I just left, and how my foster mother would dress me up so nice and call her friend out to press and curl my hair, and my foster mother would show me off to everybody. They would pinch my jaws and say how lucky I was to have parents that loved me.

I really didn't understand the god stuff and what the preacher was preaching about, and I was tired of hearing about this loving god. If he was loving, why did he allow grownups to beat children and take loved ones from each other to be separated and never know each other? How is that a loving god? I just went because I had to go. I didn't understand all that hollering and jumping up and down, talking about how he got the Holy Ghost, but I did see how my foster mother would enjoy by clapping her hands and saying amen.

We would go to church every Wednesday and Sunday. Sometimes my foster mother would ask my foster dad to go, and he would say that he was not going to give that preacher all his money and that he drove a Cadillac and that he didn't even drive nice like that. That was my father's answer, and my mother never bothered him again about going to church. My foster dad would stay home from church and watch football. She would be angry and tell my dad that he needed to give his life to God, and he would say God knew his heart and that he didn't have to be in that church to be saved or any other church. She would say that she was going to pray for him, that never stopped us from going, and she would still ask him every now and then, hoping he would change his mind and go, but he never did.

I and my roommate got ready to go. The housemother had to walk a group of us over to the gym; we couldn't go by ourselves. All the dorms were there. There were so many kids. I was shocked to see so many children. It was made up into these dorms with kids of all ages. It was a huge place, and to see all us kids in one place was amazing. Oh my god, they were all in this gym. We all had to sit on the gym floor. The preacher was a white man; him and his wife. I said to myself, "This is going to be boring."

I was ready to go back to the dorm, but as the preacher began talking about how we should talk to God, he caught my attention, saying we should make our needs known and we should talk to God like we talk to each other. As he was preaching, he stopped right in the middle of a sentence and said, "Somebody here wants to find their family," and he pointed to me out of over 200 children. He picked me out the crowd. He came down through the crowd and laid hands on me and said, "You want to find your family." I said yes, so he told me to go back to my dorm and talk to God like he was talking to me and ask him to help me find my family.

I started crying and couldn't stop. I was so overwhelmed with emotion. I couldn't control the crying, so I got up and got back in the group and I went back to the dorm and straight to my room. Then, after a few minutes, I came back out and asked Momma P, "How do you talk to God?" She told me through prayer, and then she asked me whether I knew the Lord's Prayer. I said no, and she began teaching me, but it was time for her to go home, so she said she would teach me tomorrow and every time she came to work until I learnt it. I hugged her and told her goodnight and went to my room and put my pajamas on and got on my knees and began to speak to God, and my prayer went like this, "God, I know you don't know me. My name is Barbara Hadley. I'm coming to you, asking you if you would help me find my family, my sister and brother, amen."

I crawled into bed and I started wondering if I would ever find my family or would I always be in places like this, no one to love or no one to love me. Eventually, I dozed off to sleep.

The next morning, the houseparent got us up for breakfast, and as I and my roommate were standing there, she began saying, "Girl, wasn't church good last night? I still can't believe he picked you out the crowd and told you those things about you wanting to find your family and all, you know. They say he's a prophet."

I said, "A what, a prophet? What is a prophet?"

She said, "That's someone who tells you what god says and also can predict the future. He told you that you wanted to find your family, was he right?"

"Yes, he was right."

"So, what are you going to do now?"

"I don't know. What do you think I should do?"

"Well, first, let me ask you this. Do you know your sister's and brother's names?"

"Yes."

"And can you remember the last family that your sis had?"

"Yes."

"So, what I would do is go and talk to your caseworker."

"Okay, that's what I will do. I'm going to do it after breakfast."

"Good. I'll be in the room, waiting for you. I'm praying for you."

"Thank you." I went to the houseparent that was on duty and asked her for a pass to go see my caseworker. She gave it to me and I started walking toward the building. As I started getting closer, I became nervous and my mind started racing. I began to have thoughts like, *What if she can't help? What am I going to do then?*

I made it to her office and she was in. I gave her my pass and she asked me, "What can I help you with, Barbara?" I told her that I wanted to find my family.

She said, "Okay, what can you remember about your family?"

"Well, I remember my sister, LeAnn, and my brother, Eugene. The last time I saw my sister, she was staying with a family called the Johnsons. I don't know where my brother, Eugene, is at. We were in this foster home together until Eugene ran off because the foster parent was beating us. He told me he was going for help and he would come back for me, but he never did."

"So, you said that your sister was staying with a family called the Johnsons?"

"Yes." She began to look through my files.

She said, "Yes, here are your records. Let me call the department of human services and see what I can find out." She called and they told her that my sister was still with the Johnsons. My caseworker told my sister's caseworker that LeAnn has a sister that has been looking for her.

The caseworker asked, "Is there any way that Barbara can communicate with her sister?" She told my worker that she would have to get back with her. When my worker hung up the phone, she said, "Barbara, you found your sister, and she is alive and doing well. I will make sure that you get reunited with your sister. I will not stop working on this, and I will call her back if she doesn't get back with me in a couple of days."

I said, "Thank you for helping me find her."

She said, "You're welcome," and smiled, and then I returned back to the dorm with the biggest smile on my face.

My roommate was waiting on me. She was so excited, jumping up and down, saying, "Tell me what happened. Did you find your family?"

"Yes, I found my sister. Did you know she is still with the same family that I met in Frederick, OK, the Johnson family, and she is well and doing great?"

"Are you going to be able to talk with her?"

"Maybe. My worker is working on it now." I couldn't wait to tell my favorite houseparent. It was shift change, so they were in the office, talking about what happened on the shift; they had to make daily reports.

When the houseparent came out from the meeting, she told us that it was almost lunchtime and for us to prepare and tonight was laundry night. I told Momma P that I found my blood sister, and she was so happy for me. She said I could tell her all about it later.

As we were walking to the chow hall, I couldn't stop thinking about my sister, LeAnn. I tried to picture her in my head, but I couldn't. I wondered, *Does she know where our brother is? Then we can all be together and that would be great!!!* When I was in the chow hall with all my friends, I got to thinking, *This might be my last meal here. These girls have become like family to me.*

As I was leaving the chow hall, I kept thinking about reuniting with my sister, *Is this even possible, and will she want to know me, and what will I say to her, or does she even remember me, or maybe she's not my sister.* All these things were running through my head; I began to get scared.

The houseparent called for laundry. I was the first one in line, and as I was standing there, I overheard the houseparent talking about her new pastor at her church, that his name was Rev Johnson and how he was a good pastor and that he sure could preach. I began to say to myself, *That can't be the same preacher that has my sister, it couldn't be,* so I put that thought out of my mind, and I got my laundry and went back to my room and put my clothes away and prepared for bed. I got on my knees and began to pray and asked God to bless me to be able to reunite with my sister.

Morning came, and my roommate and I prepared for breakfast. The houseparent called me to the office and told me I needed to report to my caseworker's office after breakfast. I got my pass to go, went back to my room, and told my roommate that my caseworker wanted to see me.

She said, "Barbara, that's great. She might have some news about your sister. Hurry up and get over there."

"Okay, I'm going!"

"I will be right here when you get back. I'm praying that it is good news." I got to her office as quickly as I could.

When I got there, my worker told me to sit down; she had good news for me. She said, "Barbara, your sister's caseworker contacted me and said that she talked to your sister's foster parent. She said that you all can write to each other, and this is the address. She is staying in Tulsa, and the foster parents know you."

I asked, "They know me? How do they know me?"

"I don't know, Barbara, the worker didn't tell me." My caseworker asked me whether I had ever written a letter before. I told her no, so she began teaching me. She said all I had to do was write the letter and she would mail them. I told her thank you and gave her a big hug, then I began to cry. She started crying as well.

I said, "I can't believe that I am writing my sister." I told my worker goodbye, and I ran so fast to my dorm so I could tell my best friend and roommate that me and my sister can write to each other. Who would have ever thought that this would actually be happening, that I found my sister after all these years? I asked my friend, "What should I say to my sister?"

My roommate said, "Tell her about yourself, the things you like to do, your favorite color, and ask her what she enjoys doing and what's her favorite color." So, I began writing to her, and before I knew, I was asking her to ask her foster parents could I come stay with them.

The next morning, I went to breakfast, and after breakfast I got a pass to go to my worker's office to mail my letter. She took and put a stamp on it and put it in the outgoing mail slot.

She told me, "If she writes right back, you should get a letter in two or three days." I told her thank you and I left. Well, I was waiting for my name to be called for mail, and on the third day, my name was called, and it was from my sister, LeAnn. She told me she asked her foster parents whether I could stay and they told her to tell me that I could stay because they wanted me and my sister to be reunited, and they said they will tell me how they know me and they were coming to get me real soon; they had to get the paperwork started. I told LeAnn to tell them thank you. LeAnn told me that she wanted a picture of me, so I asked Momma P to take a picture of me, and she did. I told her that my sister and I were writing to each other and I was going to live there within the same foster home. Her parents wanted me. "My blood sister. I still can't believe it I'm going to be with my sister."

"That's great, so when will you be leaving us?"

"LeAnn said when the paperwork goes through."

She said, "That's right, the paperwork." After she took my picture, she told me how pretty I was and how she loved my long hair. I was still 12 years old at this time. She began to tell me how she was going to miss me. I told her, "I'm going to miss you too, and thank you for be a friend and a mother that I never had. If it had not been for you, I would not have made it. You taught me so much, especially how to pray. Momma P, when I first came here, I didn't have any hope and I sure didn't trust anybody. Momma P, you taught that all adults are not out to hurt me and abuse children."

"Barbara, you have come a long way, and God has taken care of you and watched over you. He has made you a survivor, not a victim, so go and love your sister and new family and be good, all right?"

"I will." We hugged and shed some tears and I went back to the dorm.

When I got to my room, I got out the pen and paper and began to write my sister. My sister sent me stamps from the first letter. I began to write. When I was finished, I put my picture in the envelope and sealed it, ready to be mailed in the morning. My roommate came in and asked me what I was doing, and I told her. She said I was so blessed to have found my sister and to be able to live with her too. What a blessing.

"Now you said this is your sister that is two years older than you?"

"Yes, I am the baby. Charlotte, you know what's really bothering me?"

"What?"

"That her foster parents say they know me. How is that possible?"

"I don't know, but you will find out soon."

"Yeah, you're right."

"Come on, girl, and let me beat you on this pool table."

"Bring it on."

After we shot pool and she beat me, we went back to our room and lay down till lunch, and as I lay in my bed, I started imagining me and my sister talking and playing games with each other. *And what will we talk about? I have so much to share with her and so many questions. I wonder, does she know anything about our mother? Is it just us three blood children?* I noticed when we were in the room, my roommate would look at me and start laughing. I asked her why she was laughing and she said, "Barbara, your mind was not focused on our pool game, so I cheated. You really did beat me."

"Oh, I'm going to get you for that."

"I know, I'm sorry. It's just that you are getting better in pool than me and I was the one that taught you!" We laughed. I told her that we would have a rematch after lunch. She said okay, so we went to lunch, came back, and played pool, and I won the first game and she won the second game, then we started watching TV and went and took a nap till dinner. We went to dinner, came back, and watched TV till it was time to go to bed. I always remembered to say my prayers before going to bed.

The next morning, I got up and talked to God, asking him to let me go to a nice family, then I thought they must be nice since my sister had been with the same family for years. I wondered if my sister ever thought about me, and what did she mean that these people knew me. The thoughts were driving me crazy.

Momma P called me to the office, and when I went in there, I noticed the houseparent from the first shift hadn't gone home yet. Momma P started asking me what the names of my sister's foster parents were. "Their first names are Gerald and Ann Johnson." All of a sudden, they started shouting, "Praise the lord!!! That's them."

I asked, "Who?"

They said, "Barbara, your foster parents and sister go to our church. Your foster dad is the new pastor of our church, and your foster mother is the pianist, and your sister, LeAnn, directs the choir. They told the church family that they are getting another foster child, she is LeAnn's blood sister and she lives right here in the girls' home, and she will be with them next Sunday."

"So I'm leaving next Saturday?"

"Yes, you are."

"My sister didn't tell me that."

"Maybe she is going to tell you in the next letter, or maybe they want to surprise you."

"Are you sure that's the right pastor?"

"I'm pretty sure, Barbara, but don't get your hopes up. They have four children of their own, three girls and one boy. They are a singing family, and your sister can sing and direct a choir."

"Momma P, what am I going to do? I can't sing or direct. I barely know the Lord's Prayer. They are not going to want me. They're going to send me back," and I started crying.

Momma P said, "Barbara, they are not going to send you away because you can't sing or pray that well. Don't worry, Momma P will teach you to say grace over your food and you will learn some bible verses so they can't send you back, so we got a week; better get started."

I left her office with a smile on my face. I couldn't stop thinking that my foster dad really was a preacher right here in Taft, OK. Could it really be true that my sister is this close and I never knew it?

I began to go up to my room and pray and thank God for blessing me to find my sister and letting me be reunited with my sister. Then the houseparent called for lunchtime. She told us that she will pass out the mail early right after lunch. It was the beginning of the week, so I prayed that I would get a letter from my sister today. *I hope she has been thinking of me as much as I have been thinking of her.*

When we got back to the dorm, the houseparent called for mail call. She was calling out the other girls' names and I started getting sad, then all of a sudden she called my name. I was so excited. I ran up to get the letter and it was from my sister, and she wrote me to tell me that she and her foster parents were coming to get me to live with them this Saturday.

I ran fast as I could up to my room to tell my roommate and my best friend that they were coming to get me this Saturday. "I'm leaving. I'm leaving. Thank God I'm leaving." My roommate jumped up and hugged me and said how happy she was for me. I told her that I was praying that she would find a good home too.

She said, "Barbara, thank you." Shift change happened, and Momma P was in the office. I couldn't wait till she came out, and I let her read my letter. She did, and she said, "I'm happy that you will be with your sister and be in a good home."

"Oh my God. I don't know all the Lord's Prayer." "Don't worry," Momma P said, "you will know it before Saturday. Don't worry. Now go and shoot pool with your best friend. She is going to miss you, and we will work on the Lord's Prayer after dinner, okay?"

So, I went back to my room and asked my roommate whether she wanted to shoot some pool till dinner. "Oh yes, I will be glad to whip you before dinner." We laughed and hugged and went to the day room. She did win two games and I won one before dinner.

After dinner, Momma P and I grabbed a chair and she started working with me. I asked her, "Will I learn this prayer before Saturday?"

She said, "Yes, if you really want to learn this, Barbara, you will just listen and pay attention and try to remember what I'm telling you. I will write it all down and you study it every chance you get and you will know it before Saturday."

"Okay, I'm going to study real hard, Momma P."

She said, "Okay, I believe you. Now it's time to go to bed. I have some paperwork to do, so go in your room and don't forget to say the Lord's Prayer and also thank God for giving you a good family."

"Yes, Ma'am, goodnight, love you."

When I got to the room, Charlotte was crying. I asked her what was wrong. She told me that she found her mother and brother. I asked her how she found them, she said through her aunt. "I'm going to live with my aunt because my mother has had a nervous breakdown, so my aunt has my brother. At that time, she said she wasn't able to take care of us both, but now she is able to take care of us both financially, so you see, Barbara, I'm leaving too. God has answered both of our prayers, and looks like we both will be leaving at the same time. What a miracle!!!"

Charlotte asked if she could join me and Momma P in learning the Lord's Prayer. I said, "Sure, I will double-check with Momma P before she leaves for the night."

Before she was about to go out the door, I asked her and she said, "Sure, I will teach both of you, then you all can recite it together in your room before you go to bed."

"That's a good idea, Momma P. Thank you, and I will see you tomorrow." She said okay. I went back to my room and told Charlotte what she said, and she was happy.

So, every day that whole week, Momma P taught us the Lord's Prayer. By Friday, we knew it. We told it to Momma P and she was so proud of us. She said, "Girls, you worked very hard on the Lord's Prayer. You should be very proud of yourselves," and we were.

"Momma P, we could not have done it without you."

She said, "Girls, I was happy to do it. So keep on praying the Lord's Prayer, and you will learn other prayers, Barbara and Charlotte. Just talk to God like you are talking to me. Barbara, you have to start packing for tomorrow. The main office called and said that your foster parents and sister will be here at 3:00 p.m. to pick you up, so get packing. I will be in the office, getting your paperwork done." I said okay and then I started jumping up and down with excitement.

My roommate, Charlotte, told me she would help me pack. As we were packing my things, I began telling Charlotte that she was my first friend I ever had and she was the first person there to reach out to me and that I will never forget her and we will keep in touch. "Can you believe I've been here a year? Finally, I'm going to be with a family that loves me and also be with my blood sister, and I hope my new sisters and brother like me."

"Oh, they will. What's there to not like about you, Barbara? You keep everybody laughing, and you are sweet, and you get along well with others, so I know you will fit right on in."

"Thank you, Charlotte. I still can't believe that I'm leaving, and I sure am going to miss Momma P. She has been like a mother to me. I have learned so much from her. I will ask my foster parents if I can write to you all. We can be pen pals."

"That sounds good. I will let you know when I will be leaving, and I will give you my aunt's address. And we can let each other know how the other one is doing, okay? Friends to the end."

"Friends to the end." We hugged and kept packing up my belongings.

All that day, I was so happy. I told the houseparent on duty that my things were packed. She asked if I had anything that belonged to the group home. "If so, bring them to the office."

"Yes, Ma'am." I did have some things that belonged to the group home. I brought it to the office.

She told me to make sure that I take a shower and put something nice on and, "Let Carla in room 32 style your hair. Tell her that I told you to ask her to do your hair."

Carla was nice but shy. She could do hair real good, and every time you saw Carla, breakfast, lunch, or dinner, she was always looking nice. She was the best dressed girl in the dorm. I started picking out my clothes. I didn't know what to wear. Everything looked ugly on me. I started to get upset and thinking that I have to hide my neck. Well, I finally found something to wear.

The next morning after breakfast, I was making sure I got everything, then I got dressed and everybody said I looked nice. I got my suitcase and boxes to the day room.

This was the day that I went with my new family. I sat down, waiting for them to call the houseparent to tell me to go to the administration building. I sat there for maybe ten minutes when the call came in.

They were finally here. I grabbed my things, and in doing so I became so nervous. I walked up to the building and went in, and in seeing my sister for the first time, I didn't know what to say, so I asked her, "What you doing here?"

She said, "Silly, picking you up."

My foster dad laughed and said, "Bless your heart. Come, give me a hug. I am Rev Johnson." I felt so stupid. My sister gave me a big hug and we cried, and my foster parents cried too.

My foster mother introduced herself and grabbed my hand and said, "Come and meet your other sisters and brother." They introduced us and they told me their ages and I told them my age, and I fell in love with the baby girl, Renae. She was so cute.

My foster dad got my things and put them in the car, and I was on my way to my new life with my new family. My sister and I were just laughing and asking questions, trying to get to know each other. Dad asked if we wanted church's chicken. Everyone said yes, "So, Dad said church's chicken it is." So, we stopped and got chicken.

When we pulled up to the house, I was amazed at how beautiful it was on the outside. My brother and dad got my things out the car, and my sister grabbed my hand and we went inside. I told my sister and foster parents that the house was beautiful. They said thank you and told my sister that she and I would be sharing rooms. I was so happy to be sharing a room with my sister. She got my things and took me to her room, and we started crying again and hugging. Mom told us to wait to unpack.

"Come and eat before your food gets cold." So, we came to the table and Dad asked me to bless the food and I did. They asked me where I learned to pray like that. I told them at the girls' home, one of the houseparents there had taught me. They said that it was a beautiful prayer.

After we ate, LeAnn showed me the rest of the house. It was a four-bedroom with two bathrooms and a den; it was a big house.

Afterwards, my foster mother asked whose time it was to wash the dishes. It was my sister, Jeanette's, time. Mother said that she will have to make a new schedule and put me on it. She said she will give me time to settle in first, then I would be expected to help in the chores around the house.

I said, "Yes, Ma'am."

She said, "Go and start unpacking your things, and I will be in there in a minute to show you how to arrange your things in your dresser."

My sister, LeAnn, told me that Mother was strict, "And how she shows you how to keep your clothes, you better keep them like that or you will get the belt on your backside." That made me real nervous. And when you saw her, you could tell she was nobody to play with and that she meant business; she was a tall and stout woman.

I unpacked my things and she came in and showed me how to fold my underclothes and socks and put them away neatly, and then she said, "Barbara, I want your dresser drawer to stay neat like this, and I will be checking to make sure it stays like this."

"Okay, yes, Ma'am." I also had to make sure that I said 'yes, Ma'am' and 'No, sir' all the time in this home because they told me it was respect for your parents and they would not tolerate disrespect from their children or anybody else.

So after Mom and Dad told me that, Momma got on the piano and started playing. She played beautiful, so I came and sat down and listened to her play. She asked me whether I played or sang.

I said, "No, Ma'am, I don't know how to play or sing. I would be terrible at that."

She said, "Barbara, you can do all things through Christ who strengthens you."

I never heard that phrase before. She told me to come and sit beside her on the piano stool and she started teaching me how to sing and hold a note. She called my sisters and brother in there and they started singing, and my sister was the lead singer and my brother started playing the drums. They were a gospel group called The Johnson Family, and they were good. They were also the choir for my dad's church; what a group! I wanted to be able to sing good like my sisters.

Momma told me that, "It isn't how good you sing but what comes from your heart." She told me that, "We practice every day for an hour, so be ready, because you will be singing too." I didn't know how that was going to go, but I said okay.

When they got through practicing, my sisters and brother went in the den to watch TV. I went as well. My sisters and brother were not used to me, so I just sat there, watching whatever they were watching on TV and didn't say a word. Mom was in their room, making out the chore list, and Dad was preparing his sermon.

We watched TV for a while, and then Mom called for LeAnn to start combing the girls' hair for church.

In the morning, she called me to the room and told me that she had made out the chore list and I had dishes on Monday and I also had to vacuum the living room every day for a week. The schedule changed every week, so we started getting baths and picking out our clothes for Sunday.

Dad had started cooking Saturday's dinner. For Sunday, he was cooking a roast and mashed potatoes and green beans, with dinner rolls, and he also made a homemade apple pie. He said he made all this for me, welcoming me into the family. My brother's chores were to take out trash and mow the yard and feed the dog; the dog was a German shepherd.

When Erick went to get the lawnmower out the backyard, I asked him whether I could go with him back there to see the dog.

He said, "Sure, just let him get your scent, and pet him so he can get to know you." So I did, and he was a good dog and I loved playing with him.

I came in, took my bath, and told Momma how I enjoyed playing with Rip. She said, "That's great. Go get the comb and grease so I can press your hair." I did, and as she began combing it, she said, "I didn't believe that the picture you sent LeAnn was all your hair, but now I see that it is and it is long, thick, and beautiful hair on your head."

Well, it took Momma a long time, but I didn't mind because I loved being around her. She got it done and she put it up in a bun; it was so cute.

Dad finished cooking, and we cleaned the kitchen, and Mom and Dad retired to their bedroom, and us kids went in the den and finished watching our shows, and this time they started talking to me, asking what types of shows I liked to watch. We watched TV until it was time to go to bed. Dad came out of the room and said it was time for family prayer, so we all got on our knees in the living room and Dad prayed, and at the end, we all repeated the Lord's Prayer, and then we got up, hugged each other, and went to our rooms.

My brother, Erick, didn't even know that we had gotten up because he was asleep. Dad was mad. He raised his voice and told Erick to stop letting the devil put him to sleep every time we had family prayer. Erick said, "Yes, sir," and went to bed.

The next morning, we were awakened by my mother hollering, saying amen and praise the lord. It scared me so bad that I asked my sister what was wrong with our mother.

She said, "Nothing, she just got the holy ghost."

I said, "The holy ghost, what is that?"

She said, "I can't explain it." She told me to ask Dad, "He's the preacher." She played the piano a few minutes, and then we all started getting ready for church.

My first time at the church, Dad introduced me to the church family. They all welcomed me. When church was over, we came home and LeAnn warmed up the food, and we ate and cleaned the kitchen.

The next day, we were getting ready for school, and Mom asked LeAnn to cook breakfast. LeAnn had to cook Momma eggs a certain way, and she had a certain spoon, fork, and cup that she would eat out of, so I was watching so I wouldn't get it wrong and she be mad at me. LeAnn cooked breakfast, and we girls brought Mom and Dad's plates to them, and we cleaned the kitchen before we went to school.

Mother would teach us girls how to keep a clean house, and it had to be to her liking or you had to do it again. She told us kids that cleanliness was next to godliness, and she made sure that she instilled that in us and other things like washing one's hands before coming out the bathroom. She would even listen to see if she heard the water running. If not, she made you go wash your hands again. She talked to us about boys and how to dress and act as young ladies.

Mother would get up early in the morning, make her coffee, read her bible, and smoke her cigarettes. She and Daddy smoked; I can remember the brand of cigarettes, More Menthol 120.

We would ask to go outside and play. Momma would say, "Are all of your chores done?"

We'd say, "Yes, Mamme," and she would let us go. We would start playing kick ball, and next thing you know, all the kids in the neighborhood would come over and we'd start picking teams.

Everybody wanted my sister, LeAnn, because she could kick the ball far away, sometimes over the roof of the houses in the neighborhood. I was amazed and shocked that my sister could get the ball that far.

Momma came out and sat on the porch and watched us play. She told us whichever team won, their team would get blow pops. You see, Mom and Dad had a Sam's card. It was this big warehouse where you could buy everything in bulk. Mom and Dad would get candy, freeze pops, canned goods, tissues, and stack it in the closet. Sometimes it would be almost to the ceiling.

They would shop like that once a month because Dad said that he had a lot of mouths to feed; my dad was a hardworking man. He worked all the time; we barely spent time with him. He was either working or preparing his sermons or working on the car.

Momma, on the other hand, was a stay-at-home mom, and she spent a lot of time with us. She would play this game called trouble, sometimes she, LeAnn, and I would play jacks. She would get down on the kitchen floor and play, and she was very good at jacks; she would win all the time.

When we would play trouble, Momma sometimes would cheat, but we dare not say anything because we didn't want Momma mad at us, and it also was fun spending time with Mother.

Sometimes, on Friday, when Dad would come home early because it would be payday, Mom would have him bring church's chicken home and we wouldn't have to cook, and there was no school, so we could stay up late.

So, when we would get through eating and cleaning the kitchen, we would tell Mom and Dad that we were going to put on a show for them. They would say all right. We would dress up and, like the church members, my brother, Erick, would imitate our dad, the preacher. Mom and Dad got a kick out of it. They laughed so hard; that were just little things we did as a family.

Then we would go in the den and watch scary movies. My sisters would fall asleep and we would have to put them in the bed. My brother would be in his room, doing whatever, so it was nobody up but me and LeAnn watching all these scary movies until we got sleepy. Daddy would always tell us to make sure we turned that TV off before we went to bed. I used to love when LeAnn and I stayed up, popped popcorn in the skillet, and ate till we would get sleepy.

I would be scared to go to the room, so I would tell LeAnn to lead the way and she would say, "Why do I have to go first?"

I would say, "'Cause you are the oldest." She eventually went first. We said our prayers and jumped in the bed and covered our heads.

The next morning, when we got up, we said good morning to Mother, and, as usual, Mother was at the table with her coffee and bible. She said she liked to get up early before us kids got up so she could have her quiet time with God. So when we said good morning to Mother, that was her time to sit us down at the table and talk to us about God.

My dad would get up, get his coffee, and start looking at the bills. Mom would get upset with Dad, "And, Gerald, have faith. God will make a way for you to pay those bills. What did God say in his word? He won't put no more on you than you can bear."

Then Daddy would put the bills down and finish his coffee. Dad would then go and wake my brother up to tell him to cut the front and backyard.

My brother did not like cutting the yard, but he did it anyway, being obedient to his father and doing as he was told.

Dad would go and change the oil in the car, and then he would jack the car up and change the brake shoes. Dad was always keeping himself busy by doing something.

Momma would have us girls working on the inside, dusting, vacuuming, cleaning the icebox out because we would eat all the leftovers on Saturday so we could fit Sunday's dinner in the icebox. That was the routine in the Johnsons house because my parents didn't believe in throwing food away.

Saturday was all day cleaning, I mean general cleaning. My mother was strict when it came to cleaning. It had to be to her liking or it wasn't done right.

When we were done, Momma called for us kids to practice. We dare not say that we were tired, so we went on and did what we were told without having an attitude. Momma had us practicing on songs that we would sing on Sunday.

Just like I mentioned that we were the church choir, my dad didn't have anybody else but us, so it was mandatory that we sing and Momma play the piano and Erick play the drums; there was no one else. Dad was so proud of us being able to support him even when we were tired.

The church really enjoyed our singing and Momma playing, and to tell you the truth, I loved how they would tell us how good we could sing and that how we got invited to our churches to sing; people loved hearing us.

The only thing that really got to us kids was that when your father is a preacher, people expect his kids to be perfect. Sometimes we would get teased for our dad being a preacher, and our parents being so strict on us, we couldn't do certain things and listen to certain music, or have a boyfriend; that wasn't happening in the Johnson's house.

One day, Momma's friend's daughter came over to see us. She and LeAnn were best friends. Momma didn't mind Rose coming over because her momma and my mother sang in this gospel group called The Choir of Many Voices, so Mom and her were good friends.

Rose was way older than LeAnn, and she also had a little girl named Kiesha; she was so cute. Mom and Dad loved that little girl, and they called Rose their adopted daughter, so she was like family. She and LeAnn would go in the room and play records and talk.

Rose asked LeAnn whether she went to the movies or dated boys. LeAnn told her she wasn't allowed to do those things. "Momma and Daddy feel that it is wrong."

"So you are telling me the only thing y'all do is go to church?"

LeAnn said, "Pretty much. The only reason you get to come over is 'cause Mom and Dad know your family and know you since you were a teenager."

"I think I'm going to have a talk with Mr. and Mrs. Johnson." LeAnn was so scared because she didn't know what Rose was going to say to them, and LeAnn didn't want to be in trouble.

Rose was a very respectful young lady, and LeAnn knew if anybody could talk to Mom and Dad, it was Rose, and they would listen.

Rose went to the bedroom door and knocked; they asked who it was. Rose said, "It's me," and they said, "Come in." Rose said she wanted to talk to them and they said, "Okay, shut the door."

Momma called LeAnn to the room and they asked her what was going on. LeAnn said that, "Rose asked if I went to the movies or out on dates. I told her that I was not allowed." Dad asked LeAnn why she didn't come to them about this. LeAnn said she was scared, and she was.

Every time my sister got scared or nervous, she would rub her hands together. Mom and Dad had to tell her to put her hands down and that they were not mad or upset with her. They told her to step out the room and to tell Rose that she had to go because Dad wanted to have a talk with the whole family, so Rose left and Dad and Mom stayed in the room and talked with the door closed.

I asked LeAnn was she okay. She didn't say anything, so that let me know that she was in trouble and Momma was going to whip LeAnn, and you don't want a whipping from my mother. She would light your butt up, and my dad, when he whipped you, he would preach the bible to you while he was whipping you, and that made the whipping even longer.

Next thing you know, the door opened and Mom called LeAnn's name, and I ran to my room, and when their bedroom door closed, I went and put my ear to the door. I just heard talking and no screaming. I didn't understand, what was happening?

The door started opening, so I ran in the den with my other sisters and brother, then Dad called all of us in the dining room for a family meeting. Dad asked us that did we think that they are too strict on us and we're scared to come to them when something was on our minds. There was silence at first, then Dad said he don't want us kids to be scared to come to them about anything.

He said, "It doesn't matter how big or how small, you will not be in trouble."

My brother, Erick, spoke and said, "We want to be like other kids our age. Their parents let them go to the movies and over each other's houses, go skating, and do fun things."

Dad said, "Erick, you are right. Just because you all are a preacher's kids doesn't mean that all you kids are perfect. Even I'm not perfect, but I do want you all to hang around good kids. I am very proud of you all because you all are good kids and you don't give me or your momma any problems. You all bring in good grades; some of you are just lazy," saying no names when he said that. I knew he was talking about me.

I tried very hard at school, but most of the time I was struggling. I guess I'm what they call slow. All my sisters and brother did good on their report cards. I have had D and F on mine, and an A in gym. My worst subject was math and science; it was just hard to me; I didn't understand it at all.

One day, my sister saw me doing my homework and I started crying because I didn't understand it. She came and told me to stop crying, that she'd help me because she felt bad when Dad would yell at me because of my grades or I would get a spanking. LeAnn told me that she was going to work with me until I got it. She said no more bad grades, so she worked and worked with me until I got it, and I did get it. I was so happy, and LeAnn was happy for me as well. It was like a light went off in my head.

Well, my grades started improving, and LeAnn encouraged me so much that I made myself try harder, and I did. My mom and dad started letting LeAnn go to football games and to the movies. She was in the tenth grade, and my brother, Erick, was in the ninth grade, and I was 13, in the eighth grade.

Momma talked to us girls about boys, and my dad talked to my brother about girls. I hated when our mother would talk to us about boys because she would get too carried away and say things she shouldn't be saying, especially as a Christian, and we knew never to get caught with a boy, because you would surely be in trouble.

Momma was a tough woman, but we knew she loved us. She said she didn't want us to be like her. You see, my foster mom got married to my foster dad at 15. She didn't have much education.

You see, in those days, you could marry young. My foster dad was 23. That was a big age difference. Mom would show us pictures of her and Dad when they were young, and Dad was very handsome. Mom was pretty too.

We didn't have that much as a family, but one thing we did have was love. The caseworker would come and bring me and my sisters' new clothes. They also sent a form for Mom and Dad to fill out so we could get a voucher for new shoes.

Mom and Dad would take us to Payless and we would get two pair of shoes a piece. The state brought us clothes and sent shoe vouchers every month. We didn't have time to wear the shoes and clothes out before we got more. My sister and I had so many shoes, we didn't know what to do.

There were times when Dad didn't have money to buy his girls shoes, so we said that they could take our shoe vouchers and buy my sisters some shoes. Mom and Dad thanked us. We didn't mind because that was the right thing to do, and also we loved our little sisters.

We always pitched in to help my dad any way we could, especially us older kids, because our mother was a very sick lady. She would have blackouts and seizures, so we had to look out for Mom and sometimes take care of her because she couldn't work, so Dad had to make the living for the family.

Dad worked very hard, and there were times when I felt bad for him because sometimes the bills would be high and he would have a hard time paying them and also having to pay out of pocket for Mother's medicine. Sometimes it got to be too much, and that's when I would hear my mom and dad fussing because Dad was so stressed and tired from work and trying to stay on top with the bills.

On Fridays, I would hear Momma calling in her medicine which Dad said was very expensive, and Momma calling Dad to pick her medicine up and telling to bring home church's chicken. Even though sometimes he couldn't afford it, he did it anyway to please Momma.

Dad had her so spoiled; we didn't mind because us girls didn't have to cook on Fridays because it was church's chicken night; what a treat! We were so happy when Dad came home so we could spend time with him, but he would be so tired. After he would eat, he would go straight to sleep.

Dad was a hardworking dad. Sometimes, during the week, he would work so late, we didn't even get to see him because we would be asleep because we had to get up in the morning and go to school, so we barely saw Dad, but on the weekends, we got to spend time with him.

I can remember this one Friday night, my sister, LeAnn, and I had made some popcorn and started watching scary movies. We did this every weekend. Our sisters would always fall asleep before the movie even began, so they would go to bed and it would be only me and LeAnn up. Well, we were sitting there, watching all these scary movies until the TV went off, so we started walking down the hall. The lights were out and I was walking in front of LeAnn, and all of a sudden I saw something wearing a white gown coming down the hall. I ran and knocked LeAnn down, and LeAnn saw it too. It was short, wearing a white gown, and LeAnn asked who that was and what did it want.

Come to find out, it was our little sister, Renae. She had one of Dad's old t-shirt on. She said she wanted some water. We told her that she scared us to death. She laughed. We got her some water and she went back to bed. Dottie and I started talking in the room, and we both were wondering why our sister just stood there in the hallway and not say anything. It was puzzling, but we didn't worry about it; we just went on to bed.

The next morning, we told Mom and Dad about it, and they just laughed, and Momma said, "See, you and LeAnn better stop watching all those scary movies on the weekends. You know what happens with your baby sister when she watches the scary movie, *The Blob.* She wets the bed because she's too scared to go to the bathroom."

My birthday came around and I turned 13 years old, and Mom had made me a chocolate cake, my favorite. She invited some of the neighbors' kids over to have cake and ice cream with me. Momma had given me some perfume. She ordered from Avon. I was so happy and grateful for that because I knew we didn't have money to take me to places that give birthday parties, so Momma made it special anyway, and it was special.

We learned how to be thankful for what we had; we never complained. When I turned 13, something started happening to me. I noticed when I prayed about something, God would answer my prayer. For example, I would ask God to bless me to pass a test at school sometimes that I didn't study for, he would bless me to pass it, or I would pray that we could go to a particular place and we would go. Sometimes I would forget to do my chores and I knew if Momma found out that I would get a spanking. Well, she found out, but I just prayed that she wouldn't spank me and she didn't.

Things also started happening at night. I would see these creatures and it would scare me, and I would run and knock on my parents' door, and Dad wouldn't believe me and tell me to go back to bed, but I knew what I had seen, but they never believed me. They said I watched too many scary movies, but I wasn't watching scary movies anymore. Something was happening to me and I didn't understand what.

I went on the rest of the day doing my chores, waiting for Mom to call rehearsal. Sometimes she would buy cassette tapes and she and LeAnn would listen to the song. LeAnn would write the words down, and Momma would try to play it on the piano.

This is how we came up with new songs to rehearse. LeAnn and Momma would sometimes work on the songs for hours, and then they would call the group in to see who would lead it. My brother never led any songs. He just played the drums. Momma started working with me, leading the song. God had smiled on me. Momma played that song when I first came to them and went to church. I cried like a baby when she sang that song, and I have liked it ever since, so Momma decided that she would teach me how to sing it because it reminded me of everything I have been through and survived.

My foster parents told me that God loves me. I asked them if God loved me that much, why he allowed me to go through what I went through. My dad said, "Barbara, I don't know, but I know he allowed for a reason." My dad said that what I had been through and brought out reminded him a story in the bible, the story of Joseph, how his brothers sold him into slavery. He went from prison to the palace. My dad grabbed his bible and read me the story of Joseph and explained what the story was about.

My foster parents told me that God had a calling on my life. I didn't know what that meant, but I knew I liked the sound of God having a call on my life.

When my dad said that, I wasn't so angry with God anymore, but I never could get pass my pass, I was fearful all the time and nervous; I didn't like myself at all.

My sister, LeAnn, was always helping Mom with cooking and dressing and braiding my sisters' hair. LeAnn could cook and take care of Momma and her sister; she was great in everything; she was really smart, made straight As in school. There was nothing she couldn't do. My sisters would go to her to get their hair braided. Even though they knew I could also braid, they never came to me, just LeAnn.

I started getting angry and jealous of LeAnn because I started thinking about how she had the good life, never been moved from foster home to foster home, never been beat. While she was eating and sleeping, I was eating out the trashcan and being beaten.

So, I started for Mom's room and knocked on the door, and she said come in, and I sat down and told her how I was feeling, and then I asked her about when they said they knew me, and about that time Dad came home, so Mom said, "Barbara, let me talk to your dad and I will call you in after I have talked with your dad."

I said, "Yes, Ma'am," and shut the door behind me. They didn't take that long before they called me and LeAnn in the room and told us to sit down, and Mom said that they had something to tell me, and they said, "LeAnn, I don't know if you remember any of this; you were only four years old."

Then my dad said, "Barbara, you lived with us before. It was when we first got LeAnn, you and LeAnn came to us together."

I said, "What!" And Dad repeated it again.

LeAnn said, "I do remember that my sister was with me and then she was gone. I don't remember anything else."

Then Dad said, "LeAnn, do you remember the store we had?"

"Yes."

Then Dad said, "Barbara, you and your brother, Erick, would fight all the time, and your mother was trying to take care of you all and run the store at the same time. I would give you your toys and Erick his toys and separate y'all. You would go and take Erick's toys. You would not play with your toys. You wanted Erick's toys and y'all would fight every day. LeAnn, on the other hand, would be in the corner somewhere, playing quietly by herself. LeAnn never gave us any problems, so it got to a point that it was too much for your mother and we had to make a decision, and it was painful, but we did what we thought best and called the caseworker to come and pick you up, and we decided to keep Dottie because she never gave us any problems."

When I heard that, I got so mad and I started crying and telling Mom and Dad what I was feeling about the whole situation and how the girls loved LeAnn and not me.

Mother said, "Barbara, LeAnn has been with the girls all their life, and you just came into their lives. It is normal for them to go to LeAnn and not you. They are just getting used to you. Give them time; they will be coming to you when they get comfortable with you."

LeAnn said, "Mom is right. They will start coming when they are comfortable."

Dad said, "Okay, that's over and done with." Dad asked what we were having for dinner that night and LeAnn said that she was getting ready to make meatloaf, and Dad said, "No, you are not. Barbara is cooking tonight. LeAnn is always in the kitchen, cooking. Barbara, you never cook. The only thing you do is eat, so tonight you cook the meatloaf and cook some mashed potatoes and a vegetable."

When my dad said I had to cook and he raised his voice at me, I was so scared and nervous. I didn't know how to cook, so when Dad went to the garage, I didn't know what to do, so I put all the hamburger meat in a skillet, and about that time LeAnn came in the kitchen and said, "Barbara, what are you doing!? That is not how you make meatloaf."

I said, "LeAnn, help me!" And she started laughing, then she told me how to make it, and the dinner turned out great, and I started cooking all the time, but the fear that would come over me was overwhelming and fear still grips me to this day.

You see, I would try to learn things, but when people holler or make me feel dumb, I get frustrated and give up, and nobody ever encouraged me to keep trying, I always was afraid of failing.

Momma taught her children that the bible says we can do all things through Christ that strengthens us. I heard that all my life, but I never understood it. My sister, LeAnn, was blessed that she never had to go through what I went through.

You know, I never blamed them for being the reason that my sister and I were separated; it never bothered me because I was with her now and I didn't want to cause any trouble for us to be separated again.

I thought my life was getting better until one night I started seeing things and God started talking to me. I didn't know what was happening to me. I would say my prayers and crawl into bed, only to be woken up by an evil presence. This was the second time this had happened. I ran straight to Mom and Dad's room and banged on the door. I woke up the whole house except my sister, LeAnn. She was in the room, asleep, and she never got up.

Dad grabbed the holy oil and started praying, and when he went to approach the door, it threw my dad into the wall, then Dad started praying more and he was able to open the door and saw this evil presence over LeAnn, and he prayed it away and LeAnn never did wake up. With all us praying, LeAnn was not aware of what went on till we told her the next morning. I didn't know what was happening to me and neither did my folks. I kept having these experiences.

One time I was asleep and it was 2:00 a.m., and I got up to get some milk, and I was coming down the hallway and I heard my dad talking to God, asking God to help him pay the bills and provide for his family, and in a flash I heard something tell me to go in my secret closet and pray. I forgot about what I was coming in the kitchen for and I just did what this voice told me to do. I got in the closet and started praying for my dad, and all of a sudden I had my eyes closed and saw a bright light in the closet, and I got scared and opened my eyes and it was gone, and I jumped in the rollaway bed and dozed off, and I heard something calling my name and I opened my eyes and it was an angel at the foot of my bed, and it told me he was an angel of blessing and god had heard my prayer and that he was going to bless me 9:00 a.m. in the morning.

I tried to grab it, but my hands went straight through, and then he disappeared. I jumped up and ran to Mom and Dad's room and Dad came to the door and I told what I saw and what the angel told me. Dad just said that it was a dream and go back to bed; he didn't believe me.

The next morning, I heard Mom and Dad talking about my outbursts at night, "Now she is saying that she saw an angel and that he was going to bless her at 9:00 this morning."

About that time, I came around the corner and said, "The angel did tell me that. Why can't y'all believe me?"

Mom said, "Barbara, we can't take it anymore. We are thinking about calling the caseworker and telling her to come and pick you up, but we know that you and your sister were just reunited and we don't want to do that to LeAnn or you."

As they were talking, I kept watching the clock, and 9:00 came and the phone rung and the lady on the other end asked whether they had a foster child there named Barbara. Dad said yes, and the woman said that she was my aunt, my real mother's sister, and that she stayed in Dallas, Texas, and that she had a social-security check for me, and that she needed the address to send it to me. Dad didn't say anything for a minute, then he finally gave her the address and she hung up. Momma asked Dad who was that, and Dad couldn't say anything for a minute. It was like he was in shock. Then he said, "Barbara, you were right. She did see an angel. That was LeAnn and Barbara's aunt, and she said Barbara has a check from social security and that she is mailing it."

Momma said, "Gerald, the caseworker never told us that they knew any of LeAnn's or Barbara's relatives."

"I know that, love, that is why I am going to call the caseworker and tell her to come out here tomorrow. Ann, she said she is mailing the check out tomorrow." My sister and I started jumping up and down.

"I told you, Dad, what the angel told, and it was exactly nine o'clock."

Dad said, "You are right. I myself looked at the clock. Barbara, I'm am sorry that I didn't believe you. Now I am ready to sit down with your mother and sister, and you tell us what happened." Well, I told my family the whole story from the beginning.

The next day, the caseworker came out and Dad told her about the phone call and how the lady said she was calling from Dallas, Texas.

The worker said, "That is where LeAnn and Barbara are from." Daddy called the number when the caseworker was there and the lady that said she was our mother's sister answered and she talked and verified that it was true, that she was our blood aunt and she knew where our father was and he would be getting in touch with her. LeAnn and I were shocked that this was happening and also happy at the same time. Our mother's sister, she could tell us what happened to our mother, how she died.

LeAnn said, "Barbara, this is our blood family."

The caseworker told Dad, "If and when she sends that check, if she sends it, please don't cash it. Call me and I will let you know if she is their real aunt." Dad said okay. The worker said she was going back to the office and she would do some digging and she would get back to them when she knew something.

My foster parents went in the room, so we all went to our rooms. We knew that Mom and Dad were in there, talking, because LeAnn and I were talking.

LeAnn said, "Barbara, if this is true about this being our real mother's sister, I wonder why I didn't get a check?"

LeAnn also told me that she remembered one of mother's sisters.

I asked, "You do?"

"Yes, the one that didn't want us, that lined us up and looked us up and down and decided they didn't want me, you, or Eugene, because you with your neck, me with my cross eyes, and Eugene with his stuttering. We were considered misfits, so our mother's sister decided she didn't want us, her own blood."

Mom and Dad came out the room, and we came out, and Dad said, "What do y'all think about all this? I know that you all have been talking."

LeAnn said, "Yes, we have. I just told Barbara about how I remember one of our mother's sister, the one that didn't want us. I hope that she is not the one trying to find us, because I don't want to see her. There is so much, Barbara, that I want to tell you."

Mother said, "I will cook tonight, and, LeAnn, you take your sister in the room and share with her what you have shared with us about what you remember about your family, and I will tell your sisters not disturb you all. I will call you when dinner is ready, okay?"

Okay, so LeAnn and I went to the room. LeAnn started telling me what she remembered, and I was shocked. I couldn't believe it, but I knew my sister wouldn't make something like that up, and she was crying telling it, so I knew she wasn't making all that up, and I couldn't believe how she remembered all that; she was little too.

It answered all my questions, like how did we become children of the state. That our mother was an alcoholic and she didn't take care of us, so someone called the state on her and we were taken from our mother.

I asked LeAnn, "Do we have anymore siblings?"

She said, "Yes, you are the baby."

About that time, Jeanette, our sister, knocked on the door and said, "Momma said it's time to eat."

We said okay and washed our hands and sat down at the table with the whole family, and Dad asked was I all right, and I said, "It's a lot to take in, but I think I'll be all right."

Then Dad said, "Barbara, before you and LeAnn came to us, a white family had you all."

Momma said, "Sure did, and when we got you all, your hair wasn't combed, and, Barbara, you were starved to death. You just racked the food in your little mouth. The man you saw in Frederick, OK, was my father. He knew Mrs. Thomas because, Barbara, Lawton, OK, is my hometown, but I had no idea that Mrs. Thomas was keeping foster children, neither did my dad until that day. He was in Frederick and recognized you."

I got up from the table and went outside because I couldn't listen to no more. It made me angry all over again, and it made me mad with God, where I asked him, "Why me? Why didn't nobody want me? Not even my own mother wanted me."

My foster mother came out on the porch and hugged me and said, "Barbara, I know that you are angry and confused, but I hope you know that we love you and that we regret giving you up, especially knowing what you have been through. It breaks Momma and Dad's heart."

So, after she talked with me, she asked me to forgive her for giving me away and that it would not happen again.

"Mother, you say that, but you and Dad were going to call the caseworker just a few days ago because y'all thought I was crazy."

"I know, Barbara. Forgive me for that too, and forgive me for not believing you. Do you think you can do that for Momma?"

"I will try."

"That's all I ask, baby."

Then she kissed me and we came back in the house where I was greeted by all my sisters and they too gave me a hug, and my sister, Jeanette, said, "Barbara, I don't want to sleep in your room."

I said, "Jeanette, why not?"

Then she said, "Because I don't want God to show me nothing," and we all started laughing.

My foster dad at church started preaching on forgiveness, and after church and we got home, I asked my foster dad, "How can I forgive these people that knew I was getting beat and they did nothing but turned a blind eye? Dad, I wanted to kill them, and I still do."

He said, "Barbara, don't say things like that."

"But that is how I feel."

"I understand how you feel, and God understands how you feel too. The bible says, Barbara, if you don't forgive, God won't forgive you of your sins."

"Really?"

"Really."

"Wow, I didn't know that, Dad."

"I am so sorry that you had to go through that, and I know that your sister feels the same way, but look at you now. You are a survivor, and God has given you great testimony to help other kids and families that have been through what you've been through. You should write a book and tell your story."

Mom and Dad told me that often, but it just went in one ear and out the other. When my dad told me the story of Joseph in the bible, I realized that there was a similarity to my story and I started reading the bible, and it did make me feel better, but I was still being haunted with my past and I just struggled with the forgiveness thing.

I talked to my mom about it and she said, "Baby, it will take time, and God knows that, so just keep praying about it."

I started reading how they beat Jesus and he never did nothing to nobody; he only did good. I asked my dad why he put himself through that.

And Dad said, "For us, because he loves us. So, Barbara, if God suffered for us, he said we will have to suffer because we belong to him."

We had to constantly watch our mother with her sickness and not get her upset because she would have blackouts, the seizures.

One day, we were practicing a new song for church, and out of nowhere, Momma would have a blackout where she would start gritting her teeth and repeating the same chords on the piano. That's when we would run and get a cold towel and wipe her face, and in a few minutes she would come out of it and she would always ask what happened. And we would tell her that she had a blackout and then she'd say she wanted to lay down; it always took a lot out of her.

When Dad came in from work, we would tell Dad that Momma had a blackout today, and he would go in and visit with her and tell her to stay in the bed, and eventually she would fall asleep.

Mother was on a lot of medicine, and it was very expensive. After Momma fell asleep, Dad came out the room and started telling us when Momma's seizures had started. They started when she was pregnant with our baby sister, and when she had the baby, they stopped, but the blackouts started coming. Daddy said that when Momma and him were courting, Momma would be waiting for Dad to come over, and this particular day she saw Dad and ran to the car, grabbed the car handle, slipped, fell, and hit her head, and Dad thought that's what started her seizures. Dad told us kids not to worry or stress our mother out because that was when she would get sick.

When we would go to church, we were the choir and Momma was the pianist. Sometimes we would be at church all day because we sometimes had to go to another church that Sunday evening or we would have a program at our church and we had to sing and Momma had to play.

We would be so tired sometimes, but we couldn't let our dad down, plus we had to get up early and get our sisters and ourselves ready for school, walk them to school, and get to school ourselves; it was hard, but we did it.

I was in junior high, the eighth grade, Erick was in the ninth grade, and LeAnn was in the tenth grade.

Junior high was very hard for me; I had a problem learning, but not my brother or sister. They did well in school, especially LeAnn. She was an A student in school.

I hated when grade cards would come out, because Momma and Daddy would give out money for good grades, so when Dad came home, we would all stand around, waiting to show Dad our grade cards.

I was so nervous because my grade card wasn't good, so Momma said, "All right, the little to the biggest, show us your grade cards."

My little sisters got congratulated for theirs and got their money, then it was my turn. Dad looked at me with disappointment in his, and he pulled his belt off his waist and told me to go to the bedroom and stay there till he came. He looked at Erick's and LeAnn grade cards and told them good job and gave them their money.

He came in the room and spanked me and told me that I am not applying myself. Daddy told LeAnn to start helping me with my homework, and Dad started working with me, telling me that I can do all things through Christ who strengthens me. He also told Momma not to let me go outside till I had studied for two hours and to let LeAnn check my work, and if it was right, I could go outside to play.

Daddy was tough about education. He said once I learnt something, no one could take it from me, so I started applying myself, working real hard with my sister's help, and my grades started improving.

So, when grade cards came out, this time, I was waiting for Dad to come home, and when he did, he asked for my grade card first, and I had a big smile on my face. I went from F to B and C. He was so proud of me that he grabbed me and gave me a big hug, and then he gave me my money.

Momma was standing there, crying, because she knew how hard I had worked to bring my grades up.

Mother was always doing fun things with her children. I can remember how she would play jacks with me and LeAnn and how she would leg ten. That means she would flip her hand on the backside and catch all the jacks. That means you automatically win. It was easy for Momma to do that because she had big hands, so that is why she would beat us all the time. It didn't matter to us; we still enjoyed spending time with our mother and she enjoyed it too. That was the type of mother she was, always taking time with one of us.

You see, Momma was a stay-home mother. Dad was the breadwinner of the family and Mom stayed home and raised the children.

Dad told us kids that God intended for it to be that way, and that is how my foster parents raised us to obey the bible. Momma had an income coming in. She had LeAnn and I, her foster children, and the state sent her a check every month and furnished our medical, and clothes, and shoes. They didn't have to come out of their pocket for those things, so we were well taken care of.

Our home was a loving home. Yes, we had our share of problems like everybody else, and I remember sometimes Dad would struggle to keep the lights on, but we never knew it.

I would hear him tell Momma that God made a way out of no way. I didn't know what they were talking about, and I knew I couldn't be noisy and ask because they would tell me that this is grown folks' conversation.

On the weekends, Dad would get up, have breakfast, and get my brother up so he could cut the yard. My brother hated cutting the yard or taking out the trash. He didn't want to do anything but play with his friends in the neighborhood. Dad would say to Erick, "When you get out on your own, you are going to have to. Now these things, I'm trying to teach you responsibility, working and fixing things around the house, fixing on your own car, changing the oil and brakes, and when your washing machine breaks down, how to fix it, so you can save money, Son, you understand?"

"Yes, sir."

"Because, Son, it costs a lot of money to call a repair man out, so Dad is trying to save you money in the long run." Daddy would also call us girls out to the garage and teach us how to check the oil and transmission fluid and how to change a flat on a car and what tools to use, because he said y'all might not always have a man around who can do these things, so y'all also need to learn.

I liked when Dad was home because we could spend time with him, and he was always teaching and talking to us about being responsible.

I can remember Dad one Saturday, putting a roof on our neighbor's house, and he called us girls over there to help him because my mom had Erick in the kitchen, teaching him how to wash clothes and cook and clean, so Dad needed some help, so he had my sister, Marie, climb the ladder while he was taking off the shingles, and he told Marie how to come down the ladder, but Marie came down the wrong way and she was falling in midair. I tried to catch her, but she ended up landing in the trashcan that was in the neighbor's driveway, and she was chubby, so she got stuck, and it was a metal trashcan. We screamed for Dad and she was screaming because it was cutting her back every time Dad tried to pull her out.

Well, Momma heard Marie's screams, and by the time Momma got out there, Dad had pulled her out. Momma started fussing at Dad, telling him that we are not boys, we are girls, and stop having us do work like that.

"You should have another man helping you, not your daughters. It's too dangerous, and she could have landed in the driveway and busted her head open, so don't you ever have my girls up there again." Dad said he was sorry and he and Mom checked on Marie. I had put her in the tub, and she kept saying it hurt and she wanted Momma.

Well, Mom came in the bathroom, checked her back out, gave her a bath, and told her to dry off. She was going to put some cream on her back. Daddy also came in and checked Marie out to make sure nothing was broken, and it wasn't. She just bruised it real bad. Momma told her to go and lay down. Dad told us kids to go and play; he would do it.

You see, my mother was a tough cookie. She didn't play. My dad knew when my mother said something, she meant it, and everybody listened, especially my dad.

My dad was a peaceful man. It took a lot to get him upset, so he just went along with Momma to keep the peace and make her happy, because he didn't want to be in the doghouse, as Mom called it.

When Dad got upset, you knew it, which was very rarely, but when Dad did get upset, he would pound his fist on the table and tell Momma, "That's enough," and Momma knew he meant it, and the whole house would be silent, including Momma.

I can remember how my mother and father loved us putting on shows for them. We would dress up and act silly, and my parents would be busting their sides, laughing, and we enjoyed making them laugh.

True, my parents were Christians, but my dad taught us never let anyone run over you or invade your space or disrespect you, because Christians are still human. Never start a fight, but never back down from one either. These were just some of the values that my parents instilled in us, work hard and put back money for a rainy day, be a leader and not a follower.

I loved spending time with our dad because he had so much wisdom about everything. He would tell us about when he was a little boy and about segregation, and that he had to come in the backdoor of restaurants and drink out of the black's water fountain, and how he watched his parents go through the struggle.

Dad was very passionate about us knowing our history that he made LeAnn take black history and he told us that when we reached high school, that we had to take it too so we could understand what our ancestors went through for us to have the freedom that we do.

Sometimes Dad would get up early and wanted for us kids to get up, and he would tell us about different stories in the bible. Momma would hear him telling these stories of the bible that even she enjoyed. She would sit down and listen to my dad and then she asked my dad a question.

She said, "Gerald, why haven't you shared these stories before?"

He said, "Honey. I thought you all knew these stories. You all have your own bible, why haven't you all read them?" We didn't know what to say at that point. Dad knew we weren't reading our bible, so he told us kids to start reading the bible because there are some good stories in there. He picked us out some stories to read, and Momma asked if he could pick her out one to read, and he said, "Sure, honey," so we got our bibles and started reading. He picked me out the story of Joseph, when his brothers sold him into slavery; it was found in Genesis.

I started reading it and found myself getting angry, especially at my sister, LeAnn, wondering why she didn't have to suffer like I did, why she got to stay with the good family and I didn't. Good gosh, I was only a child, why couldn't they try harder to keep me and my sister together?

Even though I was with this family, sometimes I still felt all along and I felt like an outsider. I wondered what was wrong with me. My sister said that she understood and that she didn't hold it against me. My sister, LeAnn, was always trying to help and teach me things. She was so smart, and Momma was always calling on LeAnn for everything. She always got the credit and attention. I didn't care if I never learned because I would never add up to my sister, so I took on that 'I don't care' attitude. LeAnn always knew what to say and how to say it to get out of a whipping or get out of doing chores, because she knew how to butter up to Momma, especially when she would get in trouble; she would act so timid.

I hated when she would act like that. Not me. I was not going to let nobody run over me again. I was going to fight, and my sister was not a fighter like me because she never had to fight for anything, so I had to stand up for her. Sometimes Mom would holler at LeAnn when it wasn't her fault. If my sisters didn't do what they were told, sometimes she would blame LeAnn, and she would just stand there and take it and wouldn't defend herself. She would rub her hands together nervously and cry. That's when I would speak up for my sister and tell Momma that it wasn't LeAnn's fault.

Even though I was jealous, I still didn't let anybody hurt my sister. I always will love my sister and I will always stand up for her even though I am sometimes jealous of her, and I am not going to let anybody whip me for no reason, not me, and I knew that Mom and Dad felt that because they knew what I had been through. I vowed never again to let anyone ever mistreat me or my sister if I could help it.

All my foster parents knew I had an anger problem, because I told them, so they knew I was a ticking bomb and I think they knew how far to push me. I would tell my foster parents other things that I went through in this foster home, and I kept asking my dad, "I know that you preach a lot on forgiveness, and, Dad, I have tried to forgive my foster mother for what she's done to me, but I just can't forgive her. How do you forgive someone that has mistreated you when you have done nothing to cause them to mistreat you? Dad, I can't forgive my foster mother for what she's done to me. I will never forgive her, you hear, never!!!"

I began to cry, asking God why he allowed me to be mistreated and beaten, why? And why didn't he help me?

My sister and mom started crying, then Dad said in a trembling voice, "Baby, God was there with you. Every hit you took, God took it too, and every tear that you cried and every hurt that you felt and pain you had, God felt it too. Barbara, forgiveness is not for the other person, it's for you."

"What do you mean?"

"Barbara, when you forgive, it doesn't hurt anymore because it doesn't have power over you anymore, meaning the person. Barbara, God said if we don't forgive men for their wrongs, God won't forgive us of our wrongs."

"Oh, Dad, I will try."

When Dad got through talking with me, I started working on forgiving my foster mother and my foster sister and brother and everyone who had ever done me wrong. I knew it would be hard to do, but at least I was going to try.

The first thing I had to work on was stop being mad at God and start communicating with him, and that's where I started. I started by asking God, *Where were you when the chairs were being broken over my head? And where were you, God, when I was being beaten in the head with high-heel shoes, bleeding everywhere? And, God, where were you when she put my head through the wall?* All these questions came flooding into my mind. *Dad said, 'God, you were there.' Why did you allow her to do this to me?* I heard nothing but silence, no answer. *Dad said that you have chosen me for a special work. Why don't you speak to me!? Dad told me to speak to you and tell you how angry I am at you so I can let all this go, so talk to me!!! I'm here in my room, nobody is going to disturb us. Why?* I was in the room for hours, and I never heard anything, so I decided not to forgive. *I want her to suffer like I had to suffer and how my brother, Eugene, had to suffer at the hands of this evil person. My life has been a living hell.*

Sometimes I would think about my brother, Eugene, wondering whether he's dead or alive. LeAnn never talked about our brother, Eugene. I wondered did she want to try and find him like I found her, but I never asked how she felt; I just left it along.

Sometimes my sister, LeAnn, would catch me crying, and she would ask me what was wrong, and I would tell her I was thinking about our brother, Eugene, and that's when she would sit me down and tell me these stories about our mother.

Sometimes it was so hurtful that she would stop telling me. She said, "Barbara, I know it hurts, but I do remember our mother, and you look just like her. These stories I am telling you are the truth. Why would I want to lie about something like this?"

I said, "I believe you, LeAnn. Your nickname is Ladybug."

"And you are the baby. Because of our mother drinking, me and my other siblings were taken. It was six of us. Because my mother's sister didn't want the younger three because we were misfits, she took my older brothers and sisters. They have to be in foster care."

LeAnn would tell me stories about the time we were over at our grandparents' house and I fell in this hole, and she tried to get me out, but she couldn't and hollered for my brothers, and they came and just pulled me right on out. She said she was so amazed how strong they were; it wasn't that they were so strong, she said it was that they were order than her; she was little.

It made me mad when she told me about how our aunt picked over us like we were for auction or for sale. I thank

God for finding my sister. I was starting not to resent her, because it wasn't her fault that her foster parents let me go and kept her, and I'm glad that she didn't have to suffer like me and she was brought up in a good home.

LeAnn told me that she thanked God that she didn't have to go through what I went through, but she said she had been through a lot herself. I didn't understand what she meant, but she said, "Barbara, I have a lot of responsibilities," and she did.

LeAnn didn't get to go anywhere. She was always doing something with her sisters, making sure we didn't disturb Momma, because Momma was having blackouts more often. I was helping LeAnn too with braiding the girls' hair, getting dressed, and cooking. It was a lot to responsibility for LeAnn and I, if something went wrong, Momma would get on us older kids about why the girls' chores weren't done or why we didn't do their hair for school.

Dad would tell us when Mom was resting, "Do not let the girls disturb her, Dad's orders," and sometimes they would knock on the door, tattling on each other or us if they couldn't do a certain thing, and Mom would tell them to come in. We would try to stop them, but Momma would tell me and LeAnn that she was the mother, not us.

Mother loved buying us perfume and deodorant from Avon. She would tell us that, "A man looks at how clean you keep your body. He knows that your house will be clean also." She would always say things like that. Her favorite quote was, "Cleanliness is next to godliness," and Momma lived up to that.

She was always looking good and smelling good, and she taught our brother the same values, like cooking and cleaning and ironing, and he was good at it too. Even her dog, Rip, that was a German shepherd, was taken good care of. We had to constantly bathe him and make sure he had fresh water. Momma made sure he had his shots.

One time, I can remember Dad taking Rip to the vet and the vet told Dad that Rip had arthritis. When I heard that, I laughed so hard because I never ever heard of a dog having arthritis.

Now that beats all, so when Momma heard that, she started giving Rip his medicine and rubbing his hip, and when we would have a thunderstorm, Momma would make us go outside in the rain and untie Rip and bring him inside and make him a pallet in the laundry room; he was spoiled. Momma would have us walk him and he would be pulling us down the street.

One time, he broke from us. When we went to unlock the gate, he bolted on us. We had to catch him because we knew if we lost Rip, we better not come home, so we were running all over the neighborhood, trying to catch this dog. We finally caught him. That's just one example of our experiences with Rip, the dog.

The kids in the neighborhood used to love spending the night with us, because I guess their parents didn't have much and they saw how Momma would watch us play kick ball and how she got involved with us kids and pass blow pops and freeze pops to all the kids in the neighborhood, and the other kids' parents never got involved, so they started calling Momma Mrs. Ann and started playing with us a lot. They didn't call my parents holy roll no more because they saw that my mom and dad cared about them more than their parents did, so we all became good friends and their parents started coming over and speaking to my parents.

After a while, we all were good neighbors, and Momma started visiting their houses, and they switched numbers too. So, the parents started letting their kids spend the night and we would have a ball, but after a while, they started coming all the time, asking Momma if they could spend the night.

The girls and I started getting tired of these kids coming all the time, because they would come and eat up our food, so we talked to Mom and Dad about it, and Dad said, "I am a minister, and this is my job to help anybody I can, and some of these kids don't get the love and attention that y'all get, and didn't God tell us to love everybody?"

We said, "Yes, Dad."

"So stop being selfish and show love. Now go and play." Those were the type of parents that I had.

Mom and Dad also brought us up in a way that some people would say was strict, and they would be right, but that is how it is when your father is a preacher. Dad was the talker and counselor of the family, and Momma was the great disciplinary. He taught us to work hard for what we wanted and never cosign for anybody, not even your family.

My sister, LeAnn, and I would wear each other's clothes, while my other sisters, Marie and Renae, would argue about getting in each other's clothes. My two sisters, Marie and Renae, would argue all the time and fight.

Sometimes one of us would get in trouble, and Mom would ask who did this or said that, and we would be telling the truth, and the other person would be lying and they would not tell the truth. We would all get a whipping, and we would all be mad at the person that got us all that whipping.

Then, a week might go by, and that person would tell the truth. We would be so mad at that person, so what we would do was when Momma and Daddy would leave, we would jump on that person and tell them they better tell the truth next time and get their own whipping.

When we would tell Mom about how that person lied and that we got a whipping for nothing, Momma would say, "Well, that was a whipping that you needed and didn't get in the past."

Momma had three sisters and a brother. I never got to meet her brother. I think he had already passed when I came to live with them, but I met her three sisters, Aunt Julie, Aunt Maxi, and Aunt Vivian. They had kids, our cousins, and they were very nice, and we would play together when the aunts would visit.

Momma was the baby of her family. Aunt Julie told us that when Momma was born, she weighed 16 pounds. I couldn't believe it, but it's true. Dad brought out the newspaper clipping. She was the biggest baby ever born in that town, and she was born by a midwife. I believe that is why Momma had seizures, because lack of oxygen going to her brain. Momma was a big woman, with big feet and hands, and when she spanked you, oh boy did you feel it!!!

My dad was a little man, average height. When my Aunt Vivian would come over, sometimes Mom and Dad would pick her up, and sometimes she would catch the bus, but every time she would come, she would be a little tipsy, and Mom and Dad would take Aunt Vivian in the den and tell us to go play because they didn't want us seeing our Aunt

Vivian like that, and Mom would be getting on Aunt Vivian about her drinking, and Aunt Vivian would say, "Ann, you can't tell me nothing about my drinking. I am the older one than you."

We would come in the house and use the bathroom or have water, and we would hear Mom and her arguing. Dad would tell Momma that Aunt Vivian was too drunk to receive what she was telling her. "She's not understanding right now." We would be in the house, listening and be busting our sides, listening to Aunt Vivian. Her words would be slurred, and she would be just talking about nothing, so Dad said, "Let's take her home and talk to her when she is sober."

She told Mom that she wanted to tell her nieces and nephew bye and she wanted to give us a hug, so Momma called us in the house and Aunt Vivian gave us a hug and they took her home. Mom and her other two sisters didn't drink. They were Christians. Mom called her oldest sister on the phone and talked to her about Aunt Vivian's drinking, and Aunt Julie said that she got that drinking from their dad.

She said, "Ann, you were too little to remember Dad drinking, but I remember it."

Now when Aunt Julie and Aunt Maxi came over, they were always having Momma play the piano while they sang. Momma enjoyed being with her sisters; they would have a good time, and we had fun with Aunt Maxi's son, Josh. He was so spoiled and timid. We were always trying to make him rough, and when we roughed him up a little, he would run in the house and tell and we would get in trouble. He was always crying to Aunt Maxi, and we hated that.

Mom was also singing in a gospel group. Dad had a friend that would come down from Lawton, OK, and visit him. Dad said that they went to school together; they would get together, him, Dad, and Momma, and have a good time. He would visit us kids and tell us stories about him and Dad in school. We loved hearing those stories. He would have us laughing. He would bring us gifts and take us all out to eat. We called him uncle because he was Dad's best friend.

I can remember Aunt Maxi's ex-husband. Also how he still would come and visit Mom, but every time he came, he would spend the night with us, and in the morning Momma would cook breakfast and he would eat a dozen of eggs in one meal.

He was a big man; I couldn't believe he ate those many eggs, but he did. Mom and Dad always had friends come over to the house or spend the night.

Sometimes we didn't want anybody's kids or anybody to spend the night, because that meant they had to have our room and we would have to make pallets on the floor in the den.

People loved my mother playing at church, and there was this one church member that loved my mother and her playing. He started coming over because he loved to sing and how my mother played the piano.

I remember one time we had a 3:00 program at the church and he sang a solo for the program. Well, he started catching the Holy Ghost, and his dentures flew out his mouth and landed on this lady's lap. He didn't mind at all that he lost his teeth, he just kept right on singing. The lady didn't seem to mind either. She wrapped his teeth up and gave it to him after church.

I didn't understand much about this holy ghost that I would see people having, so sometimes I would laugh watching the little old ladies dancing around, and sometimes it would scare me when somebody would just burst out, shouting, but majority of the time it was so funny, but I dared not let Momma or Daddy see me laughing or they would have skinned me alive when we got home.

My grades started really improving because I had all the help from my teacher and at home. My brother and I were in junior high, and LeAnn was in high school, and we still had to walk our little sisters to school, but my sister, Jeanette, was her last year in elementary, so Dad said that in a couple of months that Jeanette could start walking her sisters to school and start walking home with them by herself, but Momma said no, she would walk them in the mornings and pick them up in the evenings because she said she wanted to start walking anyway, and she told Daddy that it wasn't safe for them to be walking by themselves, so Daddy said she was right, and that is what Momma started doing.

LeAnn asked Momma and Dad whether she could talk to them in the bedroom. They said yes, and so they went in the room and shut the door. LeAnn was telling them how nervous she was to be starting high school, so they talked to her, and she was okay. She even made friends; it was amazing how much my little sisters looked like their parents.

Marie was chubby and had these deep dimples, and she looked just like Dad, and Renae was Daddy's twin, she was quiet, and Jeanette looked just like her mom. People started saying that LeAnn and I looked like Mom and Dad. That made me and LeAnn feel so good inside.

All my sisters went to Lindsey Elementary, and right next to the school was a recreation center. Sometimes Mom and Dad let us walk up there if our homework and chores were done.

The name of the center was Amos T Hall. I loved going up there with my sisters and brother because they never teased me; they loved me. My brother's friends were always up there, so he got to see them and play basketball with his friends, and my sisters and I would be swinging on the swings.

Sometimes we went inside to watch my brother and his friends play basketball. We could check out any toys or games at the center as long as when we left, we turned the things back in.

All the neighborhood kids would go to Amos T Hall. It was so nice for them to have a place kids could go to stay out of trouble. We had our next-door neighbor, Mrs. Barren. She had two kids. We would always play with them because her daughter and baby boy went to the same elementary school that my sisters went to, and my sister, Jeanette, and she had the same classes, so they were good friends, so her mom and my mom became friends.

Mrs. Barren had an older son that was always in trouble. Momma told us that Paula and her brother, Ricky, could come over and we could play in the front yard because of Rip, our dog, would be trying to get out the gate.

"Right now, he is running himself to death, back and forth, along the fence, barking." Then Paula told my mom that she would ask her mom if we could come over and play in her backyard. She said she was sure her mother wouldn't mind, so she ran home and asked her mom if we sometimes could play in her backyard, and her mother came out the house and spoke to my mom and said we were welcome anytime, and then she invited my mom over for coffee in the morning while we were at school, and my mother accepted.

There were boys coming to the house to try and date my sister, LeAnn, but she wasn't interested in them. She said that they were stupid and their teeth were bad and their breath was too, and they were always coping off of her paper at school; they were not smart at all. She tried to help them and tutor them, then they tried to become her boyfriend as well. "That's why I'm not tutoring anybody else here at the house anymore, Mom." Mama laughed and told her how proud she was of her and to keep making those good grades so she could go to college.

I heard Momma and LeAnn talking and it made me mad because LeAnn was good in everything, school, cooking, singing, directing, playing the piano. There was nothing that she couldn't do. She was not afraid of anything. I wish that I was like her, so confident in herself. She would catch onto anything; if someone showed her something, she would catch on it the very first time.

My sister, LeAnn, was everything I wanted to be. The only weakness she had was she wasn't a fighter; she was timid and weak. She never stood up for herself. She let people run over her, so I had to protect my sisters, and if someone was picking on them and my brother wasn't around, they called me.

I always had the thought of people trying to do me in, so I always had a defense up. Even though I was in a Christian home, I still struggled about forgiving my foster mother that beat me. I never could forget it. No matter how hard I prayed, I just couldn't forgive; I wanted her to die. I had so much hatred for this woman and her kids. She put me and my brother through hell. The way I see it, she doesn't deserve forgiveness, she or her kids. Every time I think about it, I would get so angry inside, and then I would start crying because I would think about my brother, Eugene, wondering was he still alive.

I would talk to LeAnn about him, and she didn't seem interested in finding our brother and that made me mad, so I asked her, "Why whenever I bring up finding our brother, you change the subject or you don't seem interested?"

She said, "You know why? Because I'm mad at him for leaving you."

I told her that Eugene did a lot for me. "He took care of me and stole to feed me. I know Eugene wouldn't just leave me. Something must have happened to him." I wanted LeAnn to feel what I was feeling about our brother, but it was hard for her because she didn't go through the hell Eugene and I did, because she had parents that loved her. She didn't have to struggle with forgiveness and letting go of so much hatred for a person. I missed my brother, Eugene, and I wanted him to be in this new family that I had and that I started to care about.

Mom and Dad noticed that I was a little distant, and so they asked me what was wrong. I told them that I was thinking about my brother, Eugene. Dad said that they never told us that we had a brother, because if they had, we would have gotten him. My foster parent saw the hurt and pain in my eyes and saw how I longed for my brother and how determined I was to find him like I did LeAnn. Dad said that he remembered how he rode his bike to the store that Mom and Dad had in Lawton and Dad said that he asked him who he was and he said that he was LeAnn's brother and he wanted to talk with her, "And that's when your mom and I told him to come in, and he did. That's when we left him and LeAnn alone and your mother and I went to call the caseworker. When we came back out, Eugene was gone. We tried to keep him there, but he must have known that we were calling the caseworker because he was gone."

And Mom and Dad said that was the last time they saw my brother. My foster parents said if they would have known that Eugene was our brother, they would have kept him and we would never been apart, but that was a lie because they were the cause of LeAnn and I being separated. If my mother couldn't handle me, how was she going to put up with my brother? She would have sent him back and kept LeAnn, the perfect one, the one that does everything right and never made any mistakes.

These thoughts constantly ran through my head. I just kept all this pain inside. I tried praying, but it didn't work. *Maybe one day I can get rid of all this pain and hurt, but for now, I'll just live with it and try not to think about those times in my life that bother me, I'll just pray and you know it's working; I just won't think about it.*

I started reading my bible more and praying and I decided that I wanted to get baptized, so I told Momma and Dad. They were so happy. They sat me down and explained what it meant to be baptized.

I asked them, "Has my sister, LeAnn, been baptized?"

And they said yes. Then Momma got up and went to the room, and when she came back, she had in her hand LeAnn's baptizing papers and my other sisters' and brother's certificate.

The church that my dad preached at didn't have a baptizing pool, so he said that he would have to check with some of his friends in the ministry that had a baptizing pool and have my baptizing scheduled.

Dad would always tell me that God had a special purpose for me because everything I went through, that I should have been dead, but God allowed me to survive, "And also how he helped you remember the Johnson' name, and now here you are, sitting here with your sister; what a miracle!!! Bringing you right back to us, well, it is time for you to be baptized."

I was a little nervous because I couldn't swim. LeAnn said that I was going to be fine. She told me what was going to happen, that the preacher would say a couple of words then dunk me under the water and bring me up fast, and that was all.

As the preacher was getting ready to baptize me, he told me that they should have put in more water, but it was fine when he said his words and dunked me. My head hit the pool, but I was all right. My sister, LeAnn, was laughing so hard that she had to go to the bathroom. My sister was silly like that, and I was too. We were always laughing at something or acting silly. The preacher asked me again after the service whether I was all right. I told him that I was fine, then Dad said that God maybe was knocking some sense into me, and we all laughed. I will never forget my baptism.

Well, time went on and now I was in middle school. I made it to the 9th grade. I was so happy. LeAnn was in the 11th grade, and Erick was in the 10th. They were in high school. Every time I thought about me being in high school, I got so scared, so I talked to my sister and she told me not to worry, that she would help me like she was going to help Erick. That made me feel so much better.

Every summer, Dad signed us up for the work program so we could save our money and also help out with bills. He said this year he was signing me up so I could learn responsibility and it will teach me how to save and work ethics. I didn't believe that because I'd seen how Mom and Dad would ask Erick and LeAnn for their money all the time, and they hardly got to spend any of their paychecks, and they weren't too happy about that, especially my brother, Erick. He was always mad because Dad was taking his money, and Erick would tell Daddy that he was trying to save for a car, but they didn't care.

Dad was always drilling into our heads about work and getting a good education so we could work for ourselves and not the white man, "Because he wants to work you to death and not pay you what you are worth; he wants to keep you down." Dad said that was why he worked so much; he was trying to get ahead. Mom told Daddy to stop saying it was the white man's fault.

"It's not the white man's fault," Dad said. "Ann, you didn't grow up experiencing prejudice, I did, and what I am telling these kids is true. Blacks will never be better than whites."

I was doing great in school, and my grades were improving, and I was happy about it. One day, LeAnn came to Mother and asked if she could talk to her in the bedroom.

Mother said, "Baby, you sure can," and they went to the bedroom and shut the door. My sisters and I were wondering what they were talking about because they were in there for a long time. Finally LeAnn came out with a smile on her face. She didn't tell us what they talked about.

She just said, "Barbara, help me get dinner started." I was so curious about what they talked about and thought that my sister was going to tell me, but she didn't say anything, so I kept my mouth shut and kept preparing dinner. We sat down to eat dinner.

Sometimes we had to put Dad's plate in the oven because he would be working late, so Mom said, "Prepare his plate, and he can warm it up when he comes in." Because, you see, my dad was an insurance man, and he always had to work late around the first because that's when some of his clients would get their checks, so Dad would stay out there, working, because the more money he collected, the bigger the paycheck, so we all knew that Dad wouldn't be home until late.

We didn't mind because sometimes the first fell on the weekend and we got to stay up on the weekend, so we got to be up when Dad came home. We ate at 7 p.m. and we were finished eating around 7:45. We got the kitchen cleaned about 8:30, and Dad came home at 10:00 p.m., and we were up watching TV when he came home. We would be so happy to see him. We would run and give him a big hug, then he'd go in the room to talk to Mother and take a shower. Mom would tell me when Dad got out the shower, to warm up his food.

We always made our parents' plates and served them in the bed with their food and drink. They never had to make their plates. Mom would talk to Daddy about the day and what kind of trouble us kids got into that day. The next thing I knew, Momma was calling LeAnn to the room. Momma told her to take Dad's plate into the kitchen and come back in the room. She and Dad wanted to talk to her. She put the plate in the sink and went back in the room and shut the door. They were in there for hours. I just knew they were getting onto her about something. They was so hard on all of and us kids, especially the older kids like LeAnn. They never hardly let her have any freedom, because Momma was so sickly. She depended on LeAnn to help her with the girls, with the cooking and cleaning, and she had to sing and direct. The girls were old enough to take care of themselves now, and I could help with Momma with the cooking, but I think what it was that Momma got so used to LeAnn doing everything, and that was not fair to LeAnn.

I didn't know what was happening behind those close doors, but I did know that I was going to be there for my sister because my sister got nervous real quick and she was really timid, so I had to protect her at all cost and I was scared of no one. LeAnn never had to fight to survive like I had to, so she just let people run over her. I wasn't going to let no foster parent run over me or my sister; that's the attitude I had. If you wanted a fight, I would give you one.

Well, after two hours, she finally came out the room and, to my amazement, she was smiling, so I asked her, "What did you talk to Mom and Dad about?"

She said, "Come in the room and I will tell you."

I was so excited, I couldn't hardly compose myself, so we went in the room and shut the door, and she told me that she asked Momma and Daddy whether she could start going out on dates and to the movies.

I said, "You did what?" and she repeated it. "Oh my god! What did they say!? Tell me everything."

"Barbara, I was so nervous. I didn't know what to do."

"I know you were."

"Daddy told me to put my hands down and tell them what's on my mind. Barbara, I asked them if I could start going out to football games and to the movies and on dates, and if it is all right with them, could I start going with Wanda to places?"

Now Wanda is a friend of the family, and Wanda has this brother that LeAnn was digging. She told LeAnn that Donnie wanted to take her out, but Donnie and Wanda knew how strict our parents were. They tried to keep a tight grip on us, especially us girls. Every time Wanda came to the house, she wanted LeAnn to go to places with her, but she was too scared to ask my parents. She told LeAnn that she was 16 now and she should be going on dates, so she was the one who talked LeAnn into talking to our mom and dad, and they said that she could start taking company and going places.

Because LeAnn was a good girl and she made good grades, and Dad said she never gave them any problems, he said it was okay. Dad told Mom, "Just because I'm a preacher? These kids have to experience life just like other kids their age. No kid is perfect, and we raised them good."

Mom said, "Yes, that's true, and I have already had the talk with the girls about boys."

Dad said, "Yes, I know, so you have to talk to LeAnn about drugs and drinking, okay?" So Dad sat LeAnn down and talked to her and he said that he and Momma decided that her curfew was, on a school night, 10 p.m., and weekends 12:00 midnight. She was happy and I was happy for her, so she began going out with Wanda and her brother, Donnie, and then to football games. She would come home and tell me what a good time she had, especially with Donnie, and I enjoyed hearing all about it.

The next morning, Momma would call her into the den and question her about her date. LeAnn didn't like that. She said Momma was just being noisy, and some of the things that came out of Mom's mouth, especially when she would talk about boys with us, was shocking, and if we would have told Daddy the way Momma was talking to us girls, he would have gotten on her real bad, so we never told Dad how she was talking vulgar to us about boys.

Well, the summer was here now, and we weren't that happy about it because we knew Daddy was going to sign all us older kids up to this work program that they had for teenagers for the summer. LeAnn and Erick were already signed up, so that's all Dad was talking about.

When school was over, he was signing me up to work, so it was no fun summer for us, just work. So Dad took me down there and signed me up, and they got me the job, working with my brother at my sister's school, doing janitorial work. I was excited to be working with my brother and to be getting paid every two weeks, especially this being my first real job. Dad told me that I would have to help with the bills just like my brother and sister did.

I said, "Yes, sir." I was happy to be helping my dad out. He told me that I could pay the water bill since LeAnn helped pay the lights and Erick the gas. Daddy paid all the bills, we just pitched in. Daddy handled Momma's medicine also. Our mother was on a lot of medicines, and Dad would tell Momma it was all in her head, but she just ignored Daddy and Daddy kept buying it because he didn't want to fuss with it.

My dad was a peaceful man. He hated confrontation, but don't push my dad because he can get angry, and when he blows up, he blows up. When my mother would go to the doctor and they would tell her nothing was wrong with her and they wouldn't give her the medicine she wanted, she got angry and changed doctors. She kept changing until they gave her what she wanted. This would make Daddy so angry at Momma because he was already in debt over his head with medical bills and Momma was steadily running up bills, so they would be in the bedroom, arguing.

We didn't like to hear Mom and Dad arguing, so we tried to help Dad with Momma's medical bills and other bills he had. Momma was spoiled by Dad. He tried to give Momma everything she wanted. He did his best to make Momma happy.

If people knew what we went through as being children of a preacher and what the preacher went through, they would be surprised to know that we had problems just like them; we were not exempt just because my dad was a preacher.

My sister, Jeanette, was my foster parents' oldest blood child, and she looked just like Momma, and she was my momma's biggest challenge. Jeanette was always talking back to Momma. They couldn't get along, and Jeanette was always getting on Mother's nerves. Jeanette was stubborn and was determined to do things her way, and sometimes her mouth got her in trouble.

Marie and Renae were quiet and humble like their father. The only thing was that they would always argue with each other and that would get on Momma's nerves. I can remember them always fussing about each other wearing each other's clothes without permission. I think the reason that they fussed so much with each other was that they were so close in age.

LeAnn and I were two years apart and everybody said that we look alike. I can't see it. Even LeAnn says that I look like her. I know that we are goofy around each other. We keep each other laughing, acting silly and cracking up, and we had the strangest imagination that a person could have. Sometimes we would start laughing at the weirdest things, and LeAnn and I couldn't sit together at church because she would always make me laugh and I would get in trouble every time, so I wouldn't sit by her, but at times I had to sit by her because we sang together.

My dad was an A.M.E. pastor and we were the choir for my dad's church and were a gospel group. We went around town, singing at different churches. As growing up, I can remember Dad always pastoring these churches that barely had members, and they never had a pianist or choir, so that's when we stepped in to support our dad.

I can remember my dad preaching on Sundays so hard, like he had a lot of members, and I would ask him, "Dad, why do you preach so hard like you have a lot of members?"

He told this to me, that he is giving God his best, like he had a lot of members, and also just because we were few; they deserved a good preacher.

"Oh, I understand now, Dad."

And Dad also said that, "God called me to preach his word, not just preach my best to a big crowd. You see, Barbara, God wants your best all the time."

We all enjoyed our father when he would talk about the bible and tell us stories out of the bible, especially me. I was starting to become very interested in the bible. I wanted Dad to keep talking, but he said it was getting late and he had to get up for work, so Mom and Dad retired to their room and we ours, and we could hear them in there, laughing, watching TV, and then we saw the light go out and we knew they were asleep and it was time for us to go to bed.

Dad worked for a black newspaper; he was one of their best printers. Dad was good at his job. Sometimes Dad took us to his job. There was a man that was a janitor there named Red, and he would play and act like a little child, and I was kind of scared of him, so the next time Dad let us come with him to the job, I asked Dad, "Why does Mr. Red act like a kid instead of an adult?"

Dad said that red was a little confused in the head, "So, Barbara, don't be scared of Mr. Red. He won't hurt a fly. God has made people special like that, and God has special work for those type of people." When Dad explained it to me, I wasn't scared anymore of Mr. Red.

The school year was winding down and we were taking finals. I had studied real hard, hoping and praying that I would do good on my final tests. A week went by and it was time for finals. I went to school with a positive attitude; I was going to do my best. When the test was over, I felt that I did the best I could, so I was just waiting for the teacher to grade my test. Thank God I passed all my classes, and now I was just waiting for grade-card day.

Now that we had taken all our finals, the teachers were throwing us parties in every class; no more school work. I loved our parties. A couple of days went by, and the teacher told us that she enjoyed us being in her class, and then she passed out grade cards and let us go home early.

When I got out in the hall, I began to open my grade card and my mouth flew open because I had passed to the ninth grade. I was so happy that school was out and summer had begun and that Mom and Dad were going to be proud of me and I will get money for my grade card. I couldn't wait to get home and show Momma.

I showed Momma with a big grin on my face. Mommy was so happy that I passed and the rest of my brother and sisters also passed. Mother was so proud of all of us. She said, "I'm going to talk to your father when he gets home, and when he sees all your grade cards and see that everybody passed to the next grade, he will be so proud of all you kids. I will ask him if we can go out and celebrate. I can't promise you all, but I will see after he adds up the bills what he has left."

We said, "Okay, Momma," and went to our rooms and waited for Dad to come home, praying that Dad would have the money to take the family out.

I was so excited; I couldn't wait for Dad to get home to show him my grade card. All of a sudden, we heard Daddy's car pull up, and Mom said, "Kids, your father is home." Then she said to wait till he got settled in before we rushed him.

"Yes, Ma'am."

So, Father came in and he asked, "How my babies doing?" And he told us to come and give him a hug, and we showed him our grade cards. He was so pleased that he gave a big shout and said, "This calls for a celebration. Let's go out for pizza!!!"

We all hugged Daddy and ran and grabbed our coats and headed for the car, and while we were on our way, I told God, "Thank you for helping me pass." Mom was smiling the whole way as we told him and Mom that we loved them and they told us that they loved us too.

We were all tired and full when we got home. We went straight to our rooms and crashed out. Dad said that since school was out that we could stay up long if we kept it down and made sure we cut the TV off when we turned in, because if that TV stayed on all night, we would run up that electric bill. We said, "Yes, sir," and we told that we were not going to watch TV; we are all tired. Dad told Erick that he wanted him to get up in the morning and cut the grass because he was going to take us to sign up for summer jobs, all of us older kids, so to make sure we had that grass cut, at least the front, by 10:00 in the morning.

Erick hated cutting the grass, but he was obedient to our father, so he said, "Yes, sir."

And he told me and LeAnn to have the kitchen clean and have our choirs done by a certain time, the same time. "So make sure that you all set your alarm clocks."

We said, "Yes, sir," and went to bed.

The next morning, we heard Momma making coffee. It was about 6:00 in the morning. Momma would get up early, drink her coffee, smoke her cigarettes, and read her daily word. She did this every morning, so when LeAnn and I heard her in the kitchen, we got up and went in there and said, "Good morning, Mother."

She said, "Good morning, girls," and then she said sit down, then she started telling us what she had read in her daily word and the bible. We didn't want to be disrespectful to Mother or to God by saying that we didn't have time for bible study this morning because we knew how our mother was.

She would have us at the table for hours, so it was a good thing that we had some time to spare. We had our bible study, and Mom was happy, and we were able to get dressed and do our chores before Dad got up. I don't know how my brother did it, but he slipped past Momma without her even knowing it and started cutting the yard. My brother never seemed interested in god's word, so he tried to avoid it in every way.

One day, I asked my brother, "Hey, Erick, why is it when Dad asked you to pray at home or read a scripture in church or at home, you get mad. Don't you believe in God?"

"Barbara, it ain't that I don't believe in God. It's that Mom is constantly drilling God in our heads and that all we do is go to church and read the bible. We can't be like normal kids because we are preacher's kids. We never get a break. I have to practice playing the drums with y'all when I want to be with my friends, and if we're not practicing, I'm working. I never have any time to do what I want to do and it's not fair."

I told my brother that I understood. But what Erick didn't understand was that Mom and Dad were just doing what they thought was best for us because they didn't want us hanging around bad influences and they were trying to shield us from the outside world, picking up bad habits.

I didn't like either having such a tight rein on me because we didn't get to experience a lot of things, so it kept us wanting to experience those things. Momma was the outspoken one. She didn't pull no punches. She told us just how it was. Sometimes our mother was too outspoken, and Daddy would tell Momma that she didn't have to speak on everything that comes to her mind, and he also taught us that it's the way that you say things to people.

Dad would sometimes not say anything to Momma about how she spoke to people, and sometimes he would and Momma would be so mad, and she made Daddy pay for correcting her. She would sometimes give him the silent treatment. You could always tell when my mother didn't like something. It surely showed on her face, and sometimes she let it be known, especially with the church members, she would sometimes hurt their feelings and they would tell Daddy about what Momma said, and Daddy would get onto Momma when we got home and sometimes they would argue.

Momma didn't want to admit that she was ever wrong about anything. She was like that as well with us. Sometimes we didn't want our friends to come over because

Momma would embarrass us in front of our friends, the things she would say to our company.

When Dad got Momma home, she said that she was telling the church member the way it was. Dad told Momma that he was the pastor of the church, not her, and that it was not her place to get on a church member about anything.

Dad told Momma, "If you have a problem with what the members are doing or not doing, you should tell me about it and not handle it yourself by going to a member and getting onto them. That's my job." Then Momma told Daddy that he needs to do his job then and stop being afraid of the members by not speaking out.

We hated when Mom and Dad would fuss because it would put Momma in a bad mood and she sometimes would take it out on us kids, so we didn't bother Momma when she and Dad got into it. We stayed our distance.

Our parents taught us that a child should stay in a child's place and never speak when they weren't spoken to, and to never correct an adult or talk back when they were told to do something even if they didn't agree with it. That's the way it was in our household. Our parents taught us to respect grownups and our parents, and if you didn't, you would after they got a hold of you.

We were like every other family. The only difference? Our father was a preacher and they were strict on us, sometimes too strict, but we always had love.

The holidays were my favorite time of the year. Dad would cook, and cook he could do. You see, my dad was a cook in the army, and he could burn, if you know what I mean.

Mom and Dad told us that when he got married to Mom that he made a promise to her that he would cook on thanksgiving and Christmas and she could have a break from cooking, so, Dad, every year, cooked on holidays. He kept that promise to my mother. Oh boy did we enjoy that my dad would cook homemade apple pies from scratch and pecan pies also from scratch. It was so good. I enjoyed every bite.

The other thing I enjoyed about the holidays was all the family getting together. Momma's sisters and our cousins would come over and we would all be playing together, and Mom and her sisters would be singing and laughing and having a good time.

Christmas was the same way. I enjoyed decorating the tree, and on Christmas Eve, Dad would let us open one present and the rest we had to wait till that morning to open. We couldn't wait till morning came. My little sisters were the first ones up. They would wake up the whole house, saying merry Christmas. Well, finally Mom and Dad would come out their rooms, and Dad would pass out the presents. What a treat!!! We would run to the room to try on our new clothes.

After we modeled our clothes, Dad asked who wanted to go with him to pass out Christmas baskets to the church members. Dad said, "Whoever wants to go, start getting ready." I volunteered, and LeAnn and Momma went. The other kids stayed home. We passed out Christmas baskets every year to the church members and the shut inn. We were so thankful that we got presents. We didn't mind passing out the baskets; we actually enjoyed it.

Christmas break was now over, so we started getting ready to go back to school. I was in this typing class and I wasn't that good, but Dad had a typewriter at home, so I started practicing on it and I got better and better. Even my teacher said that I was behind at first, now I was ahead of the class. She asked me how I got so good at typing. I told her that my dad had a typewriter at home and I started practicing.

She said, "Good job, Barbara. You are doing a great job. Keep up the good work."

"My parents make me practice for two hours every day." She said good for them. She said if I kept doing what I was doing, I wouldn't have any problems passing her class. I was so happy when she told me that.

I kept practicing and I could type without looking down at the keys, and my speed was up as well. Friday, our teacher told us that we would be having a typing test, "So make sure you all practice typing and speed, and, remember, you can't look down when you are typing, so let's practice."

We practiced all that week, and now it was Friday and time for the test. The teacher set the timer and off we went. The timer went off and the test was over.

She said, "I want you all to be typing this handout while I grade all your test. I will pass the test out by the end of the class period." We practiced until she handed out the test, and I was so happy that I got a B on my typing test, and my teacher told me how proud she was of me. I smiled and said thank you.

The bell rang and school was over for the day, and I couldn't wait to show Mom and Dad my typing test, so I rushed to get on the bus and ran home. Momma was in the kitchen, cooking. I knew we were having beans and cornbread because you could smell them cooking before you hit our block. I rushed in and kissed Momma and showed her my typing test, and she gave me a big hug and told me, since I did so well on my typing test, that she would cook me my favorite dish Saturday and that was tuna casserole. I started jumping up and down with excitement. I couldn't wait till Dad got home to show him.

Dad finally made it home and I showed him, and my father said, "Barbara, I told you that you can do all things. True Christ who strengthens you. Always remember that." Then he gave me big hug. Now the only class I was struggling with was math. What a doosey! But I was glad that my sister, LeAnn, was helping me and I was getting the hang of it.

I didn't like going to school, but I knew that I had to go, so I just did what my parents instilled in me to do and that was pray, and you know what, it was working. My parents and LeAnn told me that I gave up too soon and I stopped trying, so now I worked hard at paying attention and not giving up so soon.

Daddy also told us what he used to do before a test. He had to take his drink, a glass of water. He said it cleared your mind. Dad was always giving us his wisdom on things. You see, my mom dropped out of school to marry Dad and she never went back, so she was learning with us.

Back then, in those days, you could marry early. Mom missed out on a lot of things by marrying Daddy so early in life, and she was totally dependent on Dad. She never worked. Dad had been the sole winner for the family all of

Momma's life, so there was a lot Momma couldn't help us with.

I think Momma sometimes depended on Dad too much and she put too much on him, and in my own opinion, I think that made Dad resentful because they would argue a lot. Daddy spoiled Momma. She thought she had to have everything name brand, and she would get upset with Dad if he tried to save money and buy off-brand things; nothing but the best for Mother.

I realized at an early age to be grateful for what you got and that you had to work hard to keep it. Now that I was 14, I wanted to be treated like I was 14, so I went to Momma and talked to her about what I was feeling.

She said, "Barbara, you want to be treated like a teenager, you have to start acting your age. That means assuming more responsibility around the house."

I said, "Momma, I can do that."

"LeAnn is now a senior, and she is also working full time, and one day she will want to move out, and when she does, the oldest will be next in line to help out, like she did. So, what you need to start doing is watch her and how she does things and ask her to show you because LeAnn has been with us all her life, so she knows how I like things."

So I did start helping LeAnn and she started teaching me how to do things like Mother wanted them, and it was hard at first but I soon got the hang of it. I started directing a group because sometimes we had to sing and Momma was sick, so LeAnn had to play and I directed, and thank God, we always pulled it off.

These churches that we were singing at loved us and they always wanted us to come back. Sometimes they thought LeAnn was Daddy's wife, and Daddy said, "No, this is my oldest daughter."

Sometimes Dad would take the tape recorder to church and record his sermon and us singing so Momma could listen to it when we got home, so she wouldn't miss out on the sermon or us singing. She really enjoyed it, and we also recorded so Dad could listen to his self and hear the mistakes he made preaching and we could hear the mistakes we made.

Momma would label them with the name of the church we sung at and the year; we had a lot of tapes. Sometimes we would be so wore-out from school and singing, Dad would cancel our engagements and we would rest. Momma and LeAnn really worked with me, singing and directing the group.

You had to really know what key everybody needed to be singing in and how to get the group motivated to sing. It wasn't as easy as I thought, making everyone stay on beat. All eyes are on you and that's a lot of pressure.

I'm growing up to be a young lady now, and Mom was study preaching to me about boys and learning how to keep my legs close, but sometimes I didn't want to hear it because Momma was just pounding it in us girls' head and it got to be too much sometimes. It was times that we wouldn't go to Momma and talk to her about boys.

I was glad that Mom and Dad were letting LeAnn go out on dates and to football games. She started seeing a friend of the family. The relationship didn't last long and I never knew why it ended, but I'm sure that it had something to do with Mother. LeAnn was very upset that Charles called the relationship off, but she said she understood and they would always be friends.

LeAnn just worked. She was working at this donating blood place and she was always helping out our parents. One day, she came to me and said she wanted to talk to me. I said okay, and we went in the room and shut the door. she told me that she was tired of all her money that she made going to Mom and Dad. She had to buy a lot of things that year since she was graduating. She didn't have money to help anymore on bills, "And I don't have money for my cap and gown, or money for my senior pictures or senior dues. I am the one having to pay for all that. No one else is helping me." I told her if I had it, I would help her. She said, "Baby, I know that."

So, I asked her when she was going to talk to Mom and Dad about it. She said in a few minutes. I told her that I would cook for her while she talked to Mom and Dad. She said, "Thank you, Sister."

We would do stuff like that to help each other out. My sister was not nervous at all when she knocked on their door. She was fed up with giving all her money to my parents. I had never seen my sister be so strong and it amazed me, and I was happy for her that she was speaking up for herself and she was not going to let them intimidate her anymore; she said enough is enough!!!

She went in the room and talked to them, and as I was cooking, I heard Mom raise her voice, and LeAnn raised her voice, then Dad told Mom to let LeAnn speak, and she did, and it was over and LeAnn came out and winked at me, and I smiled. I was so happy for her.

Dad told Momma that their little girl that came to them at four years old was growing up, and they had to respect her wishes, because LeAnn had always been a good kid. "She has never given us any problems, and she is a senior now, and she has a lot of things to buy. At least she is being responsible and paying for all her senior stuff and not asking us to buy it, so let her have her money; I can handle the bills."

My brother, Erick, started dating this girl named Shawn, and he bought her over to the house to introduce her to Mom and the family, Dad said she was a pretty girl and my brother really liked her, so Mom and Dad gave Erick permission for her to come over, so they would be in the den, talking, and my little sister would be peeping around the corner, making noises, bothering my brother and his company, and that made Erick mad, so he went and told Momma what my sister was doing, and Momma made them go outside and play, and she told them to stay out the den until my brother's company left. My little sisters were always bothering my sister and brother when they had company over.

This year was the last year that I would be in junior high, and I was still having problem with math. It was fractions and I just couldn't seem to get it, and I started feeling sorry for myself again. I just hated that I was not smart like LeAnn. I couldn't seem to remember what I had learned. It wouldn't stay with me.

I told LeAnn, "I think that my brain has been injured from being hit in my head so much." LeAnn told me that nothing was wrong with my head; I was just making up excuses not to focus. When she said that, it made me angry and I started yelling at her, telling her, "You don't know what I've been through. While you were living like a princess, your brother and I were going through hell."

Momma and Daddy heard me yelling and arguing with LeAnn and they came out the room, and Dad said, "What's going on?" and LeAnn told him. I was so angry, still raising my voice at LeAnn, and Momma was getting ready to say something when Dad told Momma to be quiet and let me get it out, so I did. I starting telling LeAnn while she was living with parents that loved her and eating good food, her brother and I were digging out the dumpster for food, and there were times our foster mother didn't feed us for days.

"So you don't tell me that nothing is wrong with my head 'cause you haven't been beat in the head and had chairs cracked over your head, Miss perfect." Then I went to my room and shut the door and cried. I had been holding that anger in for so long, I just exploded.

LeAnn came and knocked on the door, and I told her to come in. She sat down on the bed and just grabbed me and held me and said that she was so sorry for telling me that I was using excuses; she didn't mean to hurt me. I told her that she was right, I needed to try harder, and we hugged and cried and made up.

LeAnn asked me whether I wanted to hear more stories of our mother. I told her yes because I didn't know our mother when we got taken. I was very young too, I didn't remember anything about our mother. Some of the things she shared with me about our mother was just horrible.

You see, our birth mother was an alcoholic, and she was on it bad. LeAnn remembered this one incident when our mother came home drunk and my oldest brother, James, was holding me, and she came over to him and knocked me out of my brother's arm, and then my brother jumped up and knocked her against the wall and she slid down the wall. She told my oldest sister, Deb, to get her purse, and then she left.

I asked my sister, "Did this really happen?"

LeAnn said, "Yes. Ladybug, that was my nickname. I wouldn't lie to you." I knew in my heart that my sister wouldn't lie on our mother or to me.

I asked my sister, "Do you think that is why my neck is like this?"

She said, "Baby girl, I don't know how your neck got like that." She also said she remembered our mother taking us to bars. I started crying because I couldn't believe having a mother like this, not loving us or even wanting us.

Even after I heard all the stories, I still wanted to find our mother and ask her why. Why didn't she want us, and why would she knock me out of my brother's arms like that? Will I ever know the answers? I was 14 and still couldn't get past my past; it haunted me.

My grades started improving. I was making B's and C's. Dad said that I had come a long way in my school work, but he said he wanted those C's to turn into B's. He still felt that I wasn't applying myself enough. I told him that I was doing the best I could.

He said, "All right, at least you're passing."

I told him I would try even harder, and he said, "That's all I expect, for you to do your best."

I said, "Yes, sir."

Friday came, and I was so ready for the weekend. When I got home, I hurried up and changed out of my school clothes, got my homework done and chores, and then I asked Momma whether I could go outside, and she said yes. LeAnn asked Momma whether she could go to the football game.

That night, the two rival high schools were playing. That was one of the biggest events in our town, the high-school football on Fridays. Momma told LeAnn yes, and then LeAnn asked if she could take me. And Momma said, "I guess so. If she wants to go. Have you asked her?"

LeAnn said, "Not yet. I wanted to get the okay from you first." Mother said she appreciated that and told her to call me in the house and ask me. Well, she did, and I was so excited that Momma said I could go and that my sister wanted to take me.

I asked LeAnn, "What should I wear?"

She said, "Just wear some jeans and a blouse. You would need a jacket to wear."

I went back to my room and picked out my new jeans and blouse that the state had just sent and it came with this double belt. I looked real nice, and LeAnn did too.

Well, we were ready to go, and Daddy told LeAnn, "I will be picking you all up right here where I dropped you all off and I'll be here, waiting. I will be picking you all up at 10:00."

LeAnn said, "Yes, sir, we will be here."

Dad said, "Have a good time," and he gave us money to buy hotdogs and popcorn, then he waved and drove off.

I was so excited to be going to my first football game. I didn't know what to do. I told my sister thank you for inviting me. She said you welcome, and then we went to find a seat, and as we were looking, this guy came up to LeAnn and said hello and then he asked her who I was.

LeAnn said, "This is my sister, Barbara," and then he said, "My name is James."

I said nice to meet you, then he asked me which school did I go to and whether I had a boyfriend. LeAnn told him that I was in junior high. He kept smiling at me and I started smiling back. I felt like I was a senior, all grown up.

We went on to sit on our team's side, and he came and sat down and started talking to me, and he told me that he played on the football team as well but wasn't playing that night. It was so noisy. Everybody was yelling and standing up; it was so exciting. The best part was yet to come: half time. That's when Booker T. Washington would perform. They had the best dance and drum meager in Tulsa.

Well, we lost to Booker T, but I had a blast and I also gave James my number. I was happy but scared because I would have to see if Mom and Dad would allow him to call me. He was older than me, but one thing good about it was him and LeAnn had classes together so Mom and Dad might let me talk on the phone with him.

Dad came and picked me and LeAnn up, and we told him that we lost. He asked me whether I enjoyed going to my first football game with my sister.

I said, "Yes, I did."

When we got home, Mom called me and LeAnn to the room and she asked LeAnn how did I act, and LeAnn said real good, and then she asked me whether I met a boy. I couldn't believe she knew, so I asked her how she knew.

She said, "Mother intuition." She asked LeAnn, "Does she know this young man?"

LeAnn said, "Yes, ma'am. I have classes with him."

"So he is a senior?"

"Yes, ma'am."

Then she asked, "What is his name, Barbara?"

I said, "James, and he is on the football team, Mom, and I was wondering if he could call me."

She said, "Let me talk it over with your father and I will get back to you."

I said, "Yes, ma'am," and LeAnn and I went to our room and got our pajamas on and we talked all night till we got sleepy.

When Dad got home, it was late and I was already asleep, so the next morning, Dad was off and Mom had talked to him, and he told me to come to the room. I was so nervous that Dad was going to say no and fuss at me because LeAnn didn't get to date until 16; she just started dating. I went to their room and Dad was lying across the bed and Mom was sitting up.

He said, "Barbara, your momma told me that you met a young man at the game the other night and you would like to be able to talk to him on the phone. Is that correct?"

"Yes, sir. Mother told me that he and LeAnn have classes together and he seems to be a nice young man."

"Well, Barbara, I'm going to allow you to talk to him on the phone for only 30 minutes a day, and that's it. If you abuse this privilege, you won't get another chance, and you have to do your homework and chores first before any talking on the phone, understand?"

"Yes, sir."

"Okay, you can go call him." The reason that my dad allowed me to call my friend was that he met Momma at my age and married her, and he also was way older than Mom, so he didn't think nothing was wrong with just talking on the phone, so he allowed it.

I told Dad that he and I had exchanged numbers.

He said, "I guess you prayed that god would touch my heart so I would say yes," and he smiled. I did pray, but I didn't think God would answer so fast.

Then the phone rang and my little sister, Renae, ran to answer it, and it was James. Dad said I could talk for 15 minutes, so we did; I was so happy he called.

Dad sat us kids down and told us that he and Momma were going to make a schedule for phone time. "Because there are a lot of people living in this house and I have important calls coming in all the time, especially with me being a minister. I think I might add call waiting to the phone." I looked up to my dad because he was a hardworking man and he took good care of his family, the best he could.

Momma and Daddy figured out the phone situation and we ended up with three-way calling on the phone. Daddy said, "I have put this call waiting on the phone, and whoever is on the phone, when you hear a beep, make sure you click over even if you have to call your party back, and please do not have all three lines tied up, 'cause if you do, your phone privileges will be over. Does everybody understand?"

"Yes, sir." Then Dad asked Momma did she have anything she would like to say. She said to make sure our homework was done and our chores were done before getting on the phone, and she didn't want no fussing about the phone.

Right after Momma and Daddy finished talking to us, the phone rang and it was James. I took the call and James asked me could I ask my folks if he could come and visit me. He could only visit me on the weekends because he worked during the week right after school. I said that I would get back with him on that.

I went and knocked on Mom and Dad's bedroom door and they told me to come in, and that's when I said that James wanted to know if he could come over to meet them. Mom and Dad both said that they were wondering when he was going to get around to asking because we had been talking on the phone for a while.

Dad and Mom said, "When is a good time for him to meet with us?"

I told them that he worked during the week and he only had the weekends, so Mom and Dad said he could come over next Saturday, "So you can go and call him back and tell him that he can come next Saturday about 3:00 p.m."

I told Mom and Dad thank you and ran to call him back. He answered and said that he would be there.

Saturday morning came and I got up, did my chores, and took my shower and got dressed. My brother, Erick, was up early because he had to cut the yard, which he hated doing. Mom and Dad were also up, having their coffee. Dad was looking over the bills. He always kept the bills on the dining-room table.

Mom would complain to Dad about all those papers on the table. It would get to be too much. Dad would always tell Momma to let him clean off the table because he knew what to throw away and what not to. Momma said okay, and

Dad told Momma to tell Marie, my sister, not to touch those papers.

You see, my little sister, Marie, was always cleaning up and moving things. She was just like Momma. She liked a tidy house, but sometimes she went overboard.

Dad went through all the papers and paid all the bills, and he also cleaned the table off, and Mom was so happy. Dad then got up and went to get dressed, and then he went out to the garage and started working on his car. Erick was through cutting the backyard. Now he was getting ready to cut the front. Mom started playing the piano, and she and LeAnn started singing and working on new songs for us to sing, and then the doorbell rang and it was James. I was in the room, finishing getting ready when Mom called me and told me my company was there.

I came out the room and interdicted him to my family. Dad had already met him when he pulled up. He introduced himself and he already knew LeAnn, so Momma told him to have a seat and I sat down beside him and we talked.

Mom was watching everything, and my sisters were planted smack dab in the living room, just watching us; there was no privacy at all, and I was so upset that Momma didn't tell my little sisters to go play and let me and my company visit, but all of a sudden Dad came in through the garage and he saw what was happening and he made my sisters go outside and play, and he told Momma to go in the bedroom and give me some privacy with my company.

He told me and my company that we could visit in the den for an hour and then visiting hours would be over. I was so happy that Dad came in, so James and I visited and then he left.

Dad went in the room and talked to Momma because she got upset when Dad told her to go to the room and give me and my company some privacy. Dad told Mom that we girls were teenagers now and we were starting to take company. "You can't be in their boyfriends' faces like that, Ann. These girls are good girls. They are not going to do anything disrespectful in this house. We have to trust our kids. We know that we brought them up right, so let them be kids."

Time went on, and James kept visiting me on the weekends and we talked on the phone during the week. One weekend, James called and wanted to bring his cousin over to meet LeAnn. Mom and Dad said yes because, at that time, LeAnn wasn't seeing anybody. She and her boyfriend didn't make it because Momma ran him off.

LeAnn wasn't really looking to meet anybody then because she knew how Momma was so strict on us, but LeAnn decided to meet him anyway, so James brought his cousin over and Mom met James's cousin. Dad wasn't at home. He had to work that Saturday, so Mom said that we could visit in the den and we were having a good time. James was into karate and he was showing me and LeAnn some moves and he was demonstrating on his cousin. LeAnn and I were laughing so hard because of how his cousin was looking when James demonstrated on him. My sisters heard us laughing, then they started running back and forth, bothering us, so I called Momma and told her what my little sisters were doing. She made them go to their room and leave us alone, but then Momma came and sat down and started talking, trying to play matchmaker for LeAnn and James's cousin. LeAnn was so mad and embarrassed that she didn't know what to do and I was as well.

Momma took over the whole visit and James and I didn't get that much time to visit, and James was upset because this wasn't the first time Momma had done this, so James was tired of it, so he told me to meet him at lunch time.

He would be picking me up and we could have some lunch and alone time. I told him that I was scared and what if I didn't make it back in time for class. He told me not to worry, that he would get me back in time and nobody would know I left.

I trusted that he would get me back in time, and I couldn't wait for the next day to come and we could be alone because I really liked James and I thought about him all the time.

The next morning came, and when I woke up, James was on my mind and what we were going to do. I was nervous but excited at the same time. I got to school and I could hardly wait for that lunch bell to ring. I kept watching the clock.

Well, it finally rang, and when I got outside, James's truck was there, parked, waiting on me. I was so happy to see him. We went to get a bite to eat and he got me back to school on time. James and I started getting together every day on my lunch break for about two weeks, but one day when James came to pick me up, we didn't go to get anything to eat. He took me to this house and I asked him whose house it was. He told me it was his dad's house and we could go in and talk because his dad was at work and he had a key to his dad's house, so we went in and we started making out.

I was a virgin with no experience, so James told me to just relax, and I trusted him, so I did. After it was all over, James told me I was his now, so I went and got cleaned up, and all of a sudden I saw blood and I got scared and called James in the bathroom.

He said, "It's all right, you are a woman now."

James took me back to school and I kept thinking about what he said that I was a woman now and I was his. When school let out for the day and I was heading home, I started getting scared because I had this secret and I couldn't tell nobody. If Mom and Dad found out, they would kill me. I knew my period would be coming around soon, and when it didn't, I knew something was wrong. I got real scared. I didn't say anything to anyone. I was just praying and waiting, hoping it would come; it never did. So, I had no choice but to go to my sister, LeAnn, and tell her.

It was on a Saturday and thank God no school. LeAnn and I and my sisters had just finished our chores and Momma said we could go outside to play, but before I went outside, I took LeAnn in the room while my sisters were outside and my brother was in the garage helping Daddy change the oil in the car. I told LeAnn the whole truth and she said, "Barbara, what are you going to do, and does James know?"

I said, "I haven't talked to him."

She said, "Let me think. The first thing is to get you to the doctor, but how? I know, I will call my friend, Tara. She will know what to do, and she won't tell anybody. Let me go call her." So, LeAnn went and called her and told her the problem. She said she would get back to her and to let her make some calls. Tara came over Sunday and went to church with us, and Mom and Dad were so happy that Tara went to church that they didn't even pay attention to me and LeAnn and Tara talking. They just thought we were visiting. Tara told us that she set us up an appointment for Monday and it was free for the pregnancy test.

We were relieved that she got me a free appointment, but then LeAnn asked, "How are we going to get Barbara out of school?"

Tara said she would call the school and act like Momma and they would excuse me and her for the day. "Barbara, your appointment is for 9:00 a.m., so, LeAnn and, I will pick you all up at 8:30." We said thank you and we would be waiting. Tara visited with Mom and Dad for a minute, then she left. I had to go all that weekend, wondering if I was pregnant. What torment! I was so scared. I didn't know what to think or feel. I was just ready to get it over with, hoping and praying that I was not pregnant.

After we ate Sunday dinner, I kept thinking about Daddy's sermon on sin and if I was going to hell because I had sinned, and if I was pregnant, I knew that Mom and Dad were going to call the caseworker and send me away and once again I would be separated from my sister. I had messed up. *And if I am pregnant, what will James say? Will he be there for me, and will we raise our child?* All these thoughts were going through my head.

I finally got through eating and everybody retired to their rooms. It was my turn to do the dishes, so I cleaned the kitchen and retired to the room, and LeAnn and I talked about tomorrow, and she asked me whether I was scared. I told her yes, and she said, "Whatever happens, I am there for you because you are my blood sister and I love you, okay?" I said okay. "We are in this together."

The next morning came and I was so tired because I hadn't slept at all, so I got up and threw water on my face to try and wake up. LeAnn got up and she said, "It's going to be all right whatever happens," then her and I started getting ready for school.

After we got dressed, we had to get my little sisters up and see them off to school. My brother was always the last to get up. So, after we got everybody off to school, we told Momma goodbye and we went to the bus stop. We had to be careful when we got to school because we didn't want our brother to know what was going on.

So, at 8:30, they called me and LeAnn to the office and our brother never knew we had left school. We got to the doctor and she examined me and we were just waiting for her to come and give me the results.

When she came back in, she had them and she said there was no doubt that I was eight weeks pregnant. I started crying and we left. Tara was taking us back to school when she said, "Barbara, now that you know, you have to tell your parents, and the baby's father."

"I know."

We got back to the school and went back to class and nobody never knew what was happening but me and LeAnn. I tried to get through the rest of the day the best I could, but my mind was not focused on classwork; it was focused on me having a baby inside me. *How did this happen, and what am I going to do with a baby at age 15?*

I had some decisions to make. First, I had to tell James. *And what was he going to say? Momma and Daddy are going to kill me.* When I got home, I did my chores and homework and then I asked Momma whether I could call James. She said yes, and then I asked her, "Can I make a sandwich first?"

She looked and said, "Your appetite sure has picked up. Go ahead," and then she walked to her room and shut the door. I knew I had to hurry and tell my parents because Momma watched everything and she also was a praying woman, so I had to tell them before God did.

So I dialed James's number and he answered. I told him and he asked me had I told my parents or anybody. I said, "Yes, LeAnn knows and a friend of the family knows. She is the one that took me to the doctor. Mom and Dad don't know, or anybody else. They won't say anything; we can trust them, but what are we going to do, James?" He asked how for long I was. I told him eight weeks.

He said, "Don't worry. Meet me at lunch and we can try to figure something out." I said okay. LeAnn saw me hang up the phone, so she asked me was I talking to James and had I told him yet.

I said, "Yes, he knows, and he is coming to get me on my lunch break, and we are going to figure out how to tell our parents, so, LeAnn, don't say anything."

She said, "I won't."

The next day, I met James at lunch and he told me that he was going to tell his mother, "And then I will come over and then you and I can tell your parents together. How does that sound?"

I said, "It sounds great, but I am so scared of how my parents will react."

"I know, me too." James's mom and dad were divorced and they were still an influence in James's life, so he was more scared of what his dad would say than his mom, because all this took place in his dad's house.

James dropped me back at school before the lunch-break bell rang, and as I was coming through the doors, Mom and Dad were standing right there in the hall. I didn't know what to do. James had already drove off, thank God, because by the look on my mother's face, you knew you were in trouble. Dad told me to get my things and get in the car.

When I got in the car, LeAnn was in the car. I asked her did she tell. She said, "No, I don't know why Mom and Dad are here."

When we got home, Momma said that the counselor called and asked when my next doctor's appointment was because I didn't get excuse for the previous appointment. Mom told the counselor that she hadn't called her about any doctor's appointment. The counselor told Momma that they got a call saying that they were her and that could they be excused for a couple of hours, that she was taking me to the doctor and I would be back. Mom asked LeAnn did she know anything about this.

LeAnn said, "Yes, Mamme."

Then I said, "Momma and Dad, I am pregnant." Mom said she already knew. She said she had a dream, she just didn't say anything because she thought I would come to her if I was in trouble. Mom asked who called the school pretending to be her and who made the doctor's appointment.

LeAnn said, "Me and Tara did."

Daddy said, "I knew somebody else was involved because you all couldn't pull this off by yourselves." Daddy asked how far long I was. I told him eight weeks. "Is James the father?"

"Yes."

"Does he know?"

"Yes, and he is telling his parents as we speak."

Mom and Dad said they were very upset and disappointed in me, "But we will deal with that later. The reason that we came to the school today is to tell you that the caseworker called and that she told us that your mother is deceased. We knew that your dream was to find your mother." I didn't know what to think or feel because I never knew my mother, but LeAnn on the other hand had memories of our mother.

When I looked over at my sister, she had this blank stare on her face. I called out to her and she didn't respond, then Mom and Dad called out to her and they didn't get a response either, so they grabbed LeAnn and Momma said, "Take her to our room; she is in shock." I was so scared. I thought she was dead.

Momma put LeAnn in her arms and started praying and rocking her, and then all of a sudden she cried out and said, "My momma, no, no." It scared me so bad that the tears started to fall. She did this for at least five minutes, and then she was all right. I went and held my sister and we cried and held each other, and after a while my sister was okay. Daddy asked me whether I wanted to go back to school. Momma told Daddy to let us stay home, that we just found out that our mother was deceased. Mom and Dad knew that LeAnn and I wanted to find our mother. They told us that they would even help us, so you see how much of a shock this news was to me and LeAnn. Daddy told Momma and me that we were going to have to tell the caseworker that I was pregnant and that they would be praying that god worked this out.

"When we hear from the worker, we will let you and LeAnn know, and we will take it from there. Until then, Barbara, you are out of the choir." We were shocked when Daddy said that. Momma asked why. Dad said he would be setting a bad example for the church, "And with me being a preacher, knowing my daughter is having sex at 15 and pregnant, what example am I setting at home?" Daddy said it with so much hurt in his voice, then he said he was going back to work. Momma was upset too that I allowed this to happen, especially with all the talks she gave us girls. How could I do this to the family, and what example was I setting for my baby sisters? Not a good one. And then she went in her room and slammed the door. LeAnn looked at me with tears in her eyes and she said, "Don't worry. I graduate this year and will get us a place. You and the baby. We will not be separated again. I mean that. Never again." Then she hugged me.

The girls and Erick came in from school and Momma told them that we were having a family meeting when Dad came in from work. "He is just working till five, so go and do your homework and chores and be done when your dad gets here."

"Yes, Ma'am."

LeAnn and I didn't have any homework, but we did our chores, and as we were doing our chores, the phone rang, and it was the caseworker calling. Mom was talking to her and they talked for a while. I was looking at LeAnn, and she was looking at me. Then we just kept on doing our chores. I couldn't help but wonder, *Am I getting sent away? What are they saying about me? Maybe Momma will call me in the room after she gets off the phone with her.*

Well, Momma hung up the phone, but she never called me in the bedroom. I kept thinking about this baby. Was I going to keep it or give it away, because I didn't have any way of taking care of it. And I hadn't heard from James yet. Was he going to be there? I wondered, *Did he tell his parents, and what did they say?* I found out from my sister, Jeanette, that James had been calling, but Momma told them to tell James I was busy; she wouldn't let me talk to him.

Dad finally came home and Momma called him in the room. They talked for a while, and then they came out the room and told everybody to come and gather at the dining-room table; we were having a family meeting.

Well, Dad told the family that I was having a baby. Everybody was just staring at me. Dad said that we were going to have a baby around the house. When he said that, I looked at him; I was confused.

"That's right, Barbara. We talked to the caseworker and she wanted us to give you an abortion, but I told her that it was against our religion. Then she said that we can keep you and the baby and the assistance; they would add the baby onto the check, so we said yes."

LeAnn and I and my sisters and brother jumped up and hugged Momma and Daddy. Dad said that he was not going to be the reason again for separating too sisters. Dad said that I couldn't sing in the choir or hold any office in church and that he had to tell the assistant pastor and eventually the whole church. "I will tell the assistant pastor before church starts Sunday."

So Sunday came and Dad was talking to Rev Golden in the office, and he told Rev Golden that I was pregnant and that he had already pulled me out of the choir and he was going to use me as an example. He was going to have me stand up in front of the whole church and confess my sins. Rev Golden told Dad to not do that.

"Everybody has sinned one time or another, and as long as she has asked god to forgive her, that's all that matters, so she doesn't have to do that."

And he said, "Don't worry about the church. We love you and your family, and we will support Barbara all we can." Daddy said thank you and they hugged, and service began as usual.

After church, Rev Golden told Mom and Dad that he wanted them to come to the house to talk with them. They said okay, after church. Rev Golden ordered some chicken for us kids and his kids. He told us to play outside while the grownups talked. Rev Golden told Mom and Dad that they had to find it in their hearts to forgive me. He was glad that Rev Golden had talked to him, that it really opened his eyes, and Daddy said that, "Barbara has already been through enough, and I know she is scared. You can see it in her eyes, right, Ann?"

Momma was still upset. She didn't say too much. Well, they got through talking, and we ate and came home. Momma went straight to the room and didn't say anything.

Daddy said, "Don't worry, it's going to take her some time, but she will come around."

I was in the tenth grade now, and LeAnn had graduated from high school. She was now getting ready to go off to college. Well, I was getting so big now. My baby would be born sometime in the summer.

One day, I came in from school and Momma was talking to her friend, Betty, that she had known for a long time. Betty came over and told Momma that Shawn was also pregnant and she was going to let her go to this school for pregnant girls because she was worried that Shawn could get hurt climbing the stairs at school.

"And what if she gets knocked down by those kids running in the hallway? It's just not safe for an expecting mother." She told Momma that she should let me go to the school too, so she got all the information from her friend and said that she would talk to Dad about it.

She said, "All right, let me know because I can take them and pick them up from school; it won't be a problem."

Momma said, "Thank you. I will be calling you when I talk to Barbara and her dad."

Daddy came home and Momma called me in the room and she said, "Barbara, you know that when you came home that Mrs. Betty was here. Well, she told me that her daughter, Shawn, is also pregnant and she is letting her start going to this school for pregnant girls in a couple of weeks, and also you can have your baby at school with you after you have the baby. They have a nursery and the girls there would be taking care of your baby while you are in class. You can check on your baby anytime. I think that's a great setup. What do you think, Barbara?"

"I think it's all right."

"Well, I think you should go."

"Okay, Mom, sign me up."

So, Mom had gotten me transferred out of McClain and had me put in Margaret Hudson with Shawn. Shawn's mother picked us up and dropped us off.

The school taught us how to breathe when we go into labor and how to take care of our baby when we have it. I really did learn a lot; it wasn't that bad at all. You also got to see all these pretty babies and all these girls pregnant just like you and nobody running you over in the hallway or giving you a stank face because you are pregnant, and the classes were much smaller, and I really liked that because I got that one-on-one time with my teacher that I needed. My grades really started getting good and I was so happy about that and I knew Mom and Dad would be too.

I started getting big and the baby started moving in my stomach. It felt weird. Seemed like I was getting bigger every minute and my emotions were all over the place, because I didn't understand why Momma and Daddy were keeping James from me. The damage was already done. I believe that Mom was just trying to make me suffer for the mistake I made; he kept begging them, but the result was always the same, no! We were getting ready to see LeAnn graduate in May, and my baby was due in August, and my birthday. LeAnn only had two classes her senior year; she was so smart, it came so easy to her. Everything she did in my eyes came easy; she could cook, clean, and do our hair, and also sing and direct; what talent! Sometimes I got so angry at LeAnn. It was because I was jealous of her having the good parents that taught her and cared for her. She never had to dig in the trashcan for beer cans and sometimes for food. She was living in a nice house with a good family while I was getting beat and misused. *It just isn't fair! It just isn't fair! I hate myself.* I couldn't never understand why I had to go through what I went through; it was not my sister's fault. I knew that I loved my sister; she was my hero!

I was going through so much, I didn't know what to do with all these emotions. I wondered why I was born. My mother didn't want me. She knocked me off of my brother's lap when I was a baby; she hated me. Mom and Dad said that I survived because God had special work for me, but what was that work and when was I going to do this special work?

Dad said he will make it plain to me when he was ready, "But, Barbara, you have to work on forgiveness."

"I'm doing my best to forgive those people that made fun of me and those that knew me and my brother were getting beat and did nothing. Where was God at when this was happening to me and my brother?"

My dad said, "Barbara, God was there. Every pain that you went through, God went through. You just have to believe."

"How can I believe in something I can't see or feel?"

My dad said, "Barbara, that is what we call faith, believing in something we can't see or feel."

I started getting so big that Momma ordered my maternity clothes from the state, and when they came, I was so happy. They were very nice and comfortable, and my sisters liked them too.

My brother wasn't into things like that. He just nodded his head and walked off. My brother never really got involved in the family. He loved us, but he was a loner. He kept to himself and he never said much, because he said when he did, nobody listened, and he was always mad to do things that he didn't want to do, and Daddy wasn't home to spend time with him, so he just tried to inquire out stuff on his own or he would ask his friends' fathers, and when we would have family prayer, Erick wouldn't never pray or he would fall asleep.

Daddy would always tell Erick that he needed to get his life right with God because he was always letting the devil put him to sleep during family prayer and that he didn't even want to play the drums for the church. Erick told Daddy that he had never liked playing the drums. Even if it wasn't for the church, he didn't like playing the drums, and he never got to do anything but stay in church, and then when we got out of church, we'd come home.

"And that's all you do, drill the bible in our heads."

Daddy said, "What do you expect? I'm a preacher." Erick told Dad that he sometimes needed a father and that he was never home.

One night, Daddy came home from work. It was the first of the month and Daddy would have to work late, collecting people's insurance. He had come home and I was sleeping on the couch because the bed would hurt my back, so Mom and Dad said I could sleep on the couch, but Dad said when he came in the house that I was moaning like I was in pain, so the next morning when I got up, he told Momma and me what he heard me doing, so he told me, since I was getting close to having my baby, he wanted me to start sleeping back in the bed with my sister, LeAnn, because she could keep an eye on me if I went into labor.

One day, my sisters and I were sitting in the den, watching TV. They were sitting on the floor and I was sitting in a chair, and all of a sudden Renae said, "What was that, your stomach just jumped." I said that it was my baby moving in my stomach. They asked if they could put their hands on my stomach. So I placed their hands where the baby was kicking and they jumped with a smile on their faces, then they ran and told Momma that they felt the baby kick; they were so excited, then Momma told me to come and stand in front of her and she started talking to my belly and the baby moved and she smiled.

My sisters from that day started asking me how it felt when the baby kicked and that they couldn't wait for me to have the baby so they could play with it. It was July of 1980, and it was hot and I miserable.

I was eight months now; I couldn't wait to have this baby even though I didn't know what to expect. My teacher at the pregnancy school showed us films of child birth and that scared me to death, but I was also excited to be having my baby, something that would love me always and I would love and take care of it the best I could.

Mom and Dad were starting to be excited about the baby. They started talking more about getting prepared for its arrival.

One day, I came in from school and Mom and Dad told me to shut my eyes and I did, and when they told me to open them, I was so surprised. They had been saving up these green stamps; they had a lot of them. Well, they turned them in and were able to buy all these things for the baby. I was so happy, and they told me that they couldn't wait till the baby got there, but they never wavered from letting James come and visit me.

LeAnn had graduated and she was working so hard, trying to get prepared to go off to college. She had already spent a lot of money for her senior year. Momma and Daddy didn't have to buy nothing. She bought all her senior stuff and that made her proud. She told me that she would help me my senior year because that was a very special time and a very costly time. "It's a lot, Barbara, that you have to buy."

The fourth of July came and Dad started getting ready. He had sautéed the meat the night before, so when he got up that morning, he and Mom were already dressed. They were up, drinking their coffee and talking, and when we got up, we had gotten dressed and started cleaning.

My housework was real light. Mom told me that she didn't want me doing anything strenuous, so she said, "Barbara, I and your dad are going to go out for a minute, and while we are gone, I want you to make some potato salad for the barbeque we are having today, and I will make the bake beans when I get back."

Then Daddy told Erick to have the front yard cut by the time he got back and that he could invite his friends over for the barbeque. Erick was happy about that, so we all started on our duties while Mom and Dad left. I was so happy because we were going to have all this good food and also be able to watch the fireworks which didn't make me too happy.

Fireworks scared me. I don't like that part of the fourth of July. I think our dog, Rip, and I were in the same boat.

Momma was going to tell us to bring Rip in the garage or in the house because he was very frightened of fireworks.

Well, everything got done, and Mom and Daddy had made it back, and in their hands they had fireworks for us. We were so happy, especially my brother and little sisters. They were jumping up and down. Daddy could hardly get in the door and sit down. I told Mom that the potato salad was cooling in the icebox.

She said, "Thank you, Barbara, and girls for cleaning the house. It smells and looks great."

We loved pleasing our mother and father, it made us feel good inside. Daddy started firing up the grill, and our dog, Rip, started barking and crying so badly that Dad told Erick to bring him to the front and tie him to the tree. Dad said that he wanted to be where all the fun was and he knew that we were getting ready to barbeque and he would get the bones. Rip lay down and was so patiently watching Dad cook that meat. Every time Daddy would take it off the grill, Rip would bark and Daddy would throw him a piece.

Our neighbor down the street had two kids that we were close to. They would spend the night sometimes over at our house, so we were very close to their mom and dad, and their dad every year would make this cherry bomb and he would get out there with us kids and have firecracker wars, our family against his family. It was so much fun to watch my sisters and brother having fun. Mom would always tell our neighbor to be careful with her kids. This was the first year that I had to just be sitting down and not jumping or screaming. Momma made sure of that. She was watching me like a hawk watching a chicken, if you know what I mean. We had to bring the dog in the house. Momma made a bed for him in the laundry room and I came in and helped Momma finish making the sides for the barbeque. Everybody was barbecuing and waiting for it to get dark so they could pop their fireworks.

I started helping Momma in the kitchen, and all of a sudden she made the statement that if I hadn't gotten pregnant, I could be having fun too. Every chance Momma got, she would remind me of my mistake, but it didn't bother me anymore because my baby would be here pretty soon and I was going to be the best mother to my child.

The food was ready and we sat down to eat. Rip was so happy that he was in the laundry room and not outside. He ate and went and lay down under Momma's feet at the table. Everywhere Momma went, Rip was right behind her, shaking because he heard the firecrackers. Rip knew not to use the bathroom in the laundry room. He would go to the patio door and scratch for us to let him out, and when he was finished, he ran right to the laundry room and lay down; he was well-trained.

The next morning, Dad got all my sisters and brother up to go clean up the street. All the neighbors' kids were out there, cleaning the yard and street. The days went on by and my birthday was coming up and I also would be turning nine months. Momma and Daddy told me that I wouldn't be getting much for my birthday because they had to buy a lot of things for the baby. I didn't mind as long as my baby had what it needed. Daddy told Momma that they had to buy a car seat before the baby could leave the hospital, so that will be the next thing they said that they would buy.

Mom and Dad made it clear that they were doing this all by themselves. I thought to myself that, *If you had let James come over, he wouldn't mind at all buying for his baby. He told you all that he would take care of his baby, but you all won't let him,* so I just looked at them and didn't say anything.

My birthday finally came around and I was 16 years old. My mom and sisters made me a chocolate cake, my favorite, and Mom cooked my favorite dish, tuna casserole, what a treat.

Mom told me to close my eyes and then open them. She and Dad had bought me a camera for my birthday, and LeAnn bought me a necklace that had my name on it. Mom had also bought me some perfume and house shoes. I was so happy. It was the best birthday ever. My brother and little sisters had bought me birthday cards. Erick's birthday card had five dollars in it. I hugged everybody and told them that this was the best birthday ever.

I went to put up my things in my room, and when I walked in, there was a new gown and robe stretched out on my bed and new slippers, and there was a card saying happy birthday from Mom and Dad. It bought tears to my eyes, and when I went back into the dining room, I just grabbed Mom and Dad and hugged them real tight and cried, then my little sister said, "Stop crying," and, hugging, "and let's bring out the cake so we can eat it."

We all started laughing at Renae, then Momma said, "We're getting there, little lady, and you won't be eating no cake or ice cream before you eat your supper."

So they brought out the cake and they sang happy birthday and we sat down to eat, and then Renae had her cake and ice cream. We all sat there, talking and having a good time. After we cleaned the kitchen and everybody retired to the den and Mom and Dad went to their room and watched TV, I went to my and LeAnn's room and put all my things away, and I also went to the den to watch TV until I got sleepy and retired to the room. Mom then called me into the room and told me to wear my old robe and nightgown, that the new robe and gown was for when I went into the hospital.

I said, "Yes, Mamma," and went to bed.

The next morning, when I got up, my brother was up and he said, "Girl, your stomach is dropping. You are getting ready real soon to have my niece or nephew, and you are having your baby at the same hospital that I work at. How cool is that? Barbara, I hope that I am working when you have your baby so I can be the first to see my niece or nephew."

"I hope so too, Erick." My brother was enjoying his job as being a custodian. He told me he really enjoyed the pay because he had his own money and bought his own clothes so Mom and Dad didn't have to worry about that, and then he said, "Daddy is going to take all my money like he does LeAnn's. Barbara, I wanted to tell you that I am so sorry that Mom and Dad are keeping James from being with you and from taking care of his baby. I think it is wrong, and James would talk to me when he was at the school, and he used to ask me why Mom and Dad are keeping you from him."

I told him, "Man, I don't know."

"Well, Sis, it was nice to finally tell you how I felt. I'm on your side. Well, I got to get out of her and go to work. Talk to you later." I really enjoyed talking to my brother because he never said too much, so you never knew how he felt about things; he always kept it inside.

After Erick and I talked, I started thinking about James and what Erick had told me that James wanted to be there for me. I was also wondering did he have another girlfriend, and did he tell that girl that he had a baby on the way? I started to hurt a little bit that evening and I told Momma about it. She told me to let her know if the pains got worse.

I said, "Yes, ma'am," and went in the den and started watching TV until dinner was ready. Jeanette, my sister, was cooking spaghetti. She was 11 years old now and Mom started her cooking. My other sisters cooked stuff like hamburgers and hotdogs for now, but Momma made sure all us kids would know how to cook; even my brother was cooking. The food was ready and we fixed Mom and Dad's plate.

Mom called me to the room and asked how I was feeling. I told her that the pain hadn't gotten any worse. Dad and Mom said that my stomach had dropped a lot. They said that I was going to have the baby any day. I told Momma and Dad that the baby was moving all over the place, kicking and bawling up under my ribs and it made it sore, so I always had to move her from that position.

They laughed, then Mom said, "Go and feed my grandchild," so I left their room and fixed my plate. The food was very good that my sister had cooked.

After we all ate and we got Mom and Dad's plates, we all got in the kitchen and cleaned it up because our favorite show was about to come on. We all piled up in the den and my sister, Renae, had already grabbed me a chair, so we watched our shows and then it was time to go to bed.

Right when we were about to go to our rooms, Erick came in from work and we told him that his plate was in the oven, wrapped with foil.

He asked, "What did you all cook?" We told him that Jeanette cooked spaghetti, and he started teasing her, saying, "I'm going to die."

We all had a laugh out of it, then he knocked on Mom and Dad's door and spoke with them for a few minutes, then he went toward the kitchen. Momma hollered out and told him to wash his hands before he went in that kitchen.

He said, "Yes, Ma'am," and went and washed his hands. It was now the fourth of August, about 2:00am in the morning, and LeAnn woke me up, telling me that the bed was wet and that she was wet also. I got up and went to the bathroom and then I noticed that I couldn't stop peeing, and I told LeAnn and she woke Mom and Dad up.

Mom came in the bathroom and said, "Oh, my god, your water has broken. The baby is coming." She went in the room to get ready to take me to the hospital. She told LeAnn to give me a towel. LeAnn gave me a little face towel, and we all got dressed, and Daddy went to start the car, and Momma woke Erick up to tell him that we were going to the hospital. He said okay and went right back to sleep. When we got to the hospital, Dad was helping me out the car and LeAnn went and told the people upfront. They ran to get me a wheelchair, and as they were getting me a wheelchair, Dad said, "Barbara, you wet my back. Sit all up."

Mom said, "Gerald, she can't help that."

He said, "How am I going to get it clean?"

Momma said, "You worrying about your seat being wet instead of your daughter? Be quiet." They wheeled me up to the floor where all the babies were, and I got hooked up to all these machines, and Mom and Dad and my sister stayed a little while, and then Dad said that they were getting ready to leave because Dad had to go to work and LeAnn had to go to work. Mom and Dad said that they would bring my clothes to me when Dad got off of work. When they were getting ready to leave, the doctor came in to check me, so they stepped out for a minute, and when he was through, they asked the doctor had I dilated.

He said, "Yes, to three cm. It might be a while before this baby comes, with it being her first," so Mom and Dad kissed me and said that they would be back tomorrow.

Dad came up there, dropped my things off, and left, and they never came back. Erick was at work and he found out what room I was in, and he came to visit me and I told him that I was in so much pain, and then I asked him, "Where are Mom and Dad?"

Erick told me that they dropped my clothes off to him and they left. Erick put my clothes and personal items in the drawer and he told me that he had to get back to work but he would check on me when he went on his lunch break. "So, don't worry, Sis. I'm here and I will be here until 11 p.m. tonight." I said okay and he hugged me and left. When I had called Momma and asked her were they coming up there, she told me that Dad had to work late, then next thing I knew, Erick said that he came and just dropped off my clothes. I already felt when I was talking to Momma that she was making up an excuse for them not coming. I knew that they were teaching me another lesson for getting pregnant so young. Mom and Dad would be cool one minute, like they forgave me, and the next minute they would be cruel to me, especially Mom.

My brother that evening came back to visit me and I asked him why did he want to know if Mom and Dad came up there. He told me that he wanted me to give him James's number because he was going to call him and tell him that I was in the hospital, getting ready to have his baby.

That evening, the doctor came in and checked me and I hadn't dilated, so they gave me some medicine to make me dilate, and he said he will check back about a couple of hours, and if I hadn't moved, that they were going to give me an emergency C-section because he said that the cord might be wrapped around the baby's neck, so they would have to cut me open and take the baby out. I was terrified. He asked me was there anyone he could call for me.

I said, "Yes, my brother works here as a custodian," so I gave him Erick's name. Erick called Mom and told her what the doctor said, and she said that Dad was not home, so as soon as he'd come, they would be up there. The doctor came back after a few hours to see if the medicine had worked, and it hadn't, so they told the nurse to start prepping me for an emergency C-section. The doctor told me that he was going to get another message to my brother to tell him that I was going into surgery. They gave me this shot in my spine and told me not to move because if I did, it could paralyze me, so I stayed very still even though it hurt. Well, they wheeled me into surgery and gave me some oxygen, but I was awake the whole time. I remember that there was a sheet draped in front of me. I could hear everything, but I couldn't see anything. Then all of a sudden

I heard my baby cry. The nurse laid it right on my chest and told me it's a girl. She was so beautiful. She looked just like her dad.

They wheeled me to my room. I was out of it. Because of the medicine they gave me, I slept the rest of the night, then I was woken up by this nurse and she pushed on my stomach and the pain was so bad that I cried.

She said, "Barbara, I am sorry, but I have to do this to make sure your uterus is going down. There will be nurses coming in all during the night and day, checking your stomach, but if you get to hurting too much, let the nurses know and we can give you something for the pain."

I said, "Yes, ma'am," and she left. All during the night, they were checking me and coming in, taking my vitals, so I didn't get much sleep. The next morning, early about 6 a.m., I was woken by my baby's daddy. He had come to see me and his baby girl. I asked him how he knew I had the baby. He told me that Erick called and told him and that he better get up there before Mom and Dad came. I was so happy to see him, and he was so happy to see his little girl.

He stayed for a while, then the nurse brought the baby in and he was able to hold her. He asked me did I pick out a name for her. I said that, "LeAnn wanted to name the baby if it was a girl, so I am waiting for her to come up here and name her."

James left, but he told me that he going to go and tell his whole family, "And we will be talking again to your folks. Even if I have to take them to court, they are not going to keep me from my baby."

Later on that morning, Mom and Dad and LeAnn came to the hospital. Mom came in and asked me how I was feeling. I told them that I was very sore where they had to cut me. Mom asked Dad to step out the room so I could show her my incision. Mom and LeAnn looked at it and then Mom looked at my feet and noticed that they were swollen, so she called Daddy back in the room and told Daddy that my feet were swollen and that she wanted to talk to the doctor, so Dad went to the front and asked for the doctor. He came in and told Mom and Dad that, "Sometimes that happens when you have kids. It's nothing serious."

Mom was acting like she was so concerned, but where was she when I needed her the most? I asked the nurses to bring in the baby and they said they would because it was time for her feeding. LeAnn was so happy.

She said, "Barbara, I picked out a name for her." LeAnn told me the name and I loved it. The baby came in and everybody lit up like a Christmas tree. LeAnn was the first to hold her and feed her.

Momma was giving all the instructions on how to hold and feed a baby. I already knew because the school I was going to taught us, but I guess she was talking to Dad and LeAnn. Mom held her and burped her and talked baby talk with her, then she asked Daddy did he want to hold her.

And Dad said, "Oh no, she is too little." Mom and LeAnn played with the baby, then Dad said, "I almost forgot that we have something for you. Barbara, it's in the car. Let me go grab it." When Dad said that, I noticed the big smile on Mom and LeAnn's face.

He came back and they had bought the baby a car seat and some clothes. I was so happy!!! They stayed a little longer and then they left.

After they had left, the nurse came in and took the baby back to the nursery. She checked my uterus and told me that my uterus had gone back down to its original size and now I needed to get up and walk so I could leave the hospital. She asked me whether I was breastfeeding. I told her no, then she said, "After you do your walk, I will bring the baby back so you can feed her."

So I got up with the nurse's help and started walking. It hurt, but I did it. When I got back from walking, she asked me did I want my baby. I said yes, so they brought the baby in, and the nurse told me that, "She should not eat no more than four ounces. After two ounces, burp her." Then the nurse said, "Call me to take her back to the nursery if you want to get some sleep."

I said okay, and then the nurse left the room. I started feeding Joyce and she was so hungry that she tried to drink the whole bottle. After I fed Joyce, I told the nurse to come and get her and take her back because I wanted to get some rest. When she came and took the baby, I fell right to sleep.

I got some rest, and then I was watching TV when my sister and her friend, Dinky, came and knocked on the door. I was so happy to see my sister. Dinky asked me how I was feeling. I told him that I was feeling a lot better.

I asked LeAnn, "Do Mom and Dad know you are here and especially here with Dinky?"

She said, "Yes, I got Mom's approval. I told her that I was off today and could I bring Dinky up here to see you and my niece, and she said yes." I told LeAnn that I was happy that she came to see me. She said, "Barbara, call the nurse and have her bring me my niece."

I called down to the nursery and they said that they will be glad to bring her to me. LeAnn held her niece and fed her, and she let Dinky hold her. LeAnn said that she looked just like James.

I told LeAnn, "If I tell you something, you won't tell nobody, will you?"

She said, "No, Barbara, I won't. What is it?" I told her that James had seen his baby girl. "What, how did that happen?"

I said, "Erick. When I had the baby that night, Erick called James and told him. He came the next morning early to see his baby."

LeAnn said, "Barbara, that is good. I asked Momma were they going to buy a baby bed. They said that they are going to let James buy the bed, so, Barbara, maybe they have forgiven him."

I said, "That's great. I hope they have." LeAnn asked me how I felt being a mother. I said great. LeAnn said, "Barbara, she is our blood. She is a Hadley, and I'm going to be the best aunt I can be." LeAnn told me that she was off that weekend and she was going to ask Momma and Dad if she could spend the night with me since I go home tomorrow.

I said, "LeAnn, that would be great!!!"

So she did just that and Mom and Dad said she could and to call them when they discharged me. LeAnn said she would. Momma asked LeAnn whether Dinky was still up there. LeAnn said yes. She asked to speak to him. LeAnn was so nervous because she didn't know what Momma was going to say.

Dinky got off the phone and LeAnn asked him, "What did Momma want to talk to you about?"

Dinky said, "Nothing, she just told me thank you for bringing you up here and to tell my mother she said hello, that's it." We were shocked. Momma was trying to change.

Well, Dinky had to go, and the nurse had come in and told me that I needed to walk so I could go home tomorrow, so LeAnn helped me and we walked together down to the nursery to see all those pretty babies and also to see our baby. She was sleeping, so beautiful.

We didn't want to disturb her, so we walked back to the room, and when we got back, LeAnn started braiding my hair, and then the doctor came in and checked me and said I could go home tomorrow with my baby. He said my baby was fine; she had gained two pounds. LeAnn and I were so happy because I had been in the hospital a week and I was ready to go home.

They had brought my dinner in, so LeAnn said that she was going to the cafeteria to get herself something to eat while I was eating my dinner. While I was eating my dinner, there was a knock on the door. It was the whole family. Everybody came to see me; I was so surprised. I started crying when I saw my little sisters and my brother. About that time, LeAnn walked through the door and she also was surprised. Momma told me that the reason they hadn't been up there was because she had been sick and Daddy had been working late. LeAnn gave me this look like to say that Momma wasn't telling the truth why she hadn't been up there, but I didn't care; they were there now. Momma asked everybody to leave the room so she could check my feet, so everybody left the room while Momma checked me out. I loved the attention Momma was giving me. I felt that she really cared. Then Momma was saying that the room was dirty and asked whether I had a bath today. I said no, so Momma called the nurse and complained that the room was dirty and she wanted somebody to give me a bath.

Daddy said, "Barbara, you know how your mother is. She is just looking out for her baby." I guess. The housekeeping people came in and the nurse said that I would get a bath when my guests left. Momma said to the nurse that she appreciated that and could she bring the baby to the room. The nurse told Momma yes and have a good day.

The baby came and my sisters were so excited. They asked me if they could hold her. I said yes. Mom was telling my sisters how to hold the baby and make sure they held her head. Mom got the baby and changed her and fed her, and then she started talking to the baby and the baby started trying to talk back, and Momma was so excited; she loved her grandchild. I told Dad that I was going to discharge at 11 in the morning. Dad said he would be there. Mom had brought me clothes for tomorrow, and she also brought the baby's clothes. Dad told Momma that they were getting ready to go and he would be there in the morning. They kissed Joyce and me, and then Momma told me to keep my feet elevated. I said, "Yes, Ma'am," and then LeAnn said she was leaving so I could get my bath and also get some rest, but she said that she would come with Dad to pick me up. LeAnn said that she loved me and she will see me in the morning. I told her that I loved her too and I would see them in the morning.

I called the nursery and asked them could they come get the baby. They did, and then I called the nurse and asked her if she could give me some medicine because I was hurting. She said that she would be right there. When she came in, she went on and took my vitals and said that after I woke up, she would give me my bath. I said okay. After about five minutes, I started feeling the medicine kick in and I couldn't hardly hold my eyes open; I was out like a light. The nurse was still coming in, taking my vitals, but I didn't mind, I was feeling really good.

When I woke up from nap, I rung the nurse and asked her could I have my bath now. She said she was on her way. I got everything together for my bath.

When she came in, I was ready to go, so she told me that she was going to walk with me and get me in the shower. She said I was doing great walking on my own, but it was the hospital policy that she stayed with me, so she stood outside the door and waited till I got through, then she walked me back to my room and helped me get back in the bed. She asked me did I need anything for pain. I told her not until after I fed my baby and spent time with her, because we were going home tomorrow, so she called housekeeping in to change my sheets while she got the baby. Housekeeping had changed my sheets and emptied my trash and then she left the room, and as she was leaving out, the baby was coming in.

I fed her and changed her and started playing with her, then she fell asleep and I put her in her bed and kept her in the room with me. I started watching TV and then I fell back to sleep. I guess that bath did it, that and the fresh sheets.

When I woke up and looked at the time, I noticed that the baby had been in the room all evening. I called down at the nursery to tell them to come and get her. I told them that she slept through her feeding and changing. They told me that they will take care of it and they took her. I got out of bed and started getting our things together for us to leave tomorrow. I couldn't believe that I had slept this long. The day was almost over with and I hadn't gotten my or Joyce's things together to leave in the morning, so it put me in a frantic state, so I was rushing around the room like a chicken with his head cut off, trying to get things together.

I finally got everything together, and when I got finished, I was ready for my pain medicine, but, instead, the people came with my dinner, so I decided to wait to call for my pain medicine until I ate. When I got through eating, the nurse brought me my pain medicine and I didn't wake up till the next morning when they brought me my breakfast.

I ate and asked if they could bring my baby so I could feed her. They did, and when she came, she was already waiting for her momma to feed her. She had her eyes wide open. I fed her and played with her. I told the nurse that she will not be going back to the nursery because we are going home today. The nurse said she will be getting her bottles and diapers and everything else I needed for her to discharge. I told the nurse thank you. I started getting myself together while Joyce was sleeping, then I got Joyce together. She was so cute and still knocked out, asleep.

Dad and LeAnn came. Momma was not with them. I got all the paperwork done and I left the hospital. LeAnn got Joyce in her car seat and we were off.

When we got to the house, Dad open the door and Momma took the baby from LeAnn and started giving her a bath. She didn't say nothing to me till she was through. After that, Momma started trying to take over the baby and Dad had to tell Momma that the baby was mine, not hers. Momma told Daddy to be quiet. She was trying to teach me how to take care of her grandchild. Momma got through bathing Joyce and ran her straight to her room and started putting lotion and powder on her.

She said, "Barbara, you have to work fast because she is cold." She put Joyce's new clothes on her and combed her hair; she was so cute and she smelled so good. Momma took over from then on. As I look back now on the whole situation, I thank God for Momma because she taught me how to take care of my baby.

Joyce became everybody's pride and joy; even my brother started spoiling her. The baby was majority of the time in Mom and Dad's room. Dad told Momma, "We are going to have to talk to Barbara and James together so we can see what their plans are for raising this baby. It is time for us to let James be a part of his child life."

Momma said, "I know, but I don't like him."

Dad said, "Ann, you don't even know him, so give the boy a chance. So, honey, call Barbara in and let her put the baby in her room. She is asleep, and have her call James and see if he can come over."

Well, Momma called for me to come and put the baby in the room, and Dad told me after I laid her down to come back in there. I did what Daddy said and came back in the room. Dad talked to me and told me to go and call James and see if he could come over, that they wanted to talk to us together. I was so happy that Mom and Dad finally wanted to talk to James. I prayed that when I dial his number, he would be there. I hadn't seen or talked to him since the baby was born.

The phone rung and James picked up. He was so surprised to be hearing from me. I told him that Mom and Dad wanted to know if he could come over and we all talk. James said that he was going to ask his mother to come too because she wanted to see the baby to make sure that before I take care of a baby, she makes sure that she is mine. I told Momma that she was mine, that she looked just like me. James told me to hold on for a minute while he asked his mother will she go with him, she said yes, "So, Barbara, I will call you back when we are coming."

I told Mom and Dad what James said, and Momma said that she hopes when they want to come that it is a time when my father is there so we both can talk with him and his mother and get some understanding. "Yes, Ma'am." Joyce woke up from her nap, so I asked to be excused. They said yes, so I went to the room to get my little girl, and Momma started telling me how to take care of her. She started telling me to make sure that I'm not overfeeding her. She showed me how to wash and sterilize her bottles.

"If you don't stop Joyce, she will drink all four oz. of her bottle. I know she loves to eat."

Daddy laughed and said, "Yeah, just like her momma."

An hour had passed and the phone rang. It was James and he wanted to speak with Dad, so I told Dad that it was James and he wanted to speak with him. Dad came to the phone. Dad said that it would be fine and he would see them in a few. Dad hung up. He told me and Momma that James and his mother were on the way over.

Mom said, "Okay, you better get the baby ready." I changed the baby's clothes and brushed her hair. I was so happy that she was going to see her dad and grandma.

The knock came at the door and it was James and his mom. James introduced his mom to my mom and dad, then Dad told them to come in and have a seat. I spoke to his mom and she asked if she could see my baby. Mom told me to go get the baby.

I did, and soon as she saw Joyce, she said in a flash, "Oh yeah, this is my grandchild. She looks just like you, James," and smiled. James then got his daughter from his momma and started kissing her. Dad asked James was he going to take care of his baby.

James said, "Yes, what does she need?" Momma hurried up and said a baby bed. James said that he would pick one up this Friday. Mom and Dad said that he can come on these days to see the baby and not try to spend time with me; they made that clear.

The summer was almost over with and school was getting ready to start. I'm in the tenth grade now, and LeAnn was getting ready to go off to college. I was so nervous about high school and having a baby to take care of, but I knew I could do it. LeAnn said she would help me all she could. I went back to the doctor and he took out my staples and told me that I was healing fine.

Mom and Dad started discussing about who would keep the baby while I went to school. Momma came up with the idea of Momma watching Joyce as long as LeAnn paid her.

So the next thing I knew, Momma was calling me and LeAnn to the room and told us her idea. I couldn't believe it, and LeAnn couldn't believe it either. LeAnn had this look on her face that I will never forget. She was mad at Mom for even suggesting an idea like that. "This is your grandchild, and you going to charge to keep her." I told LeAnn that I didn't want her doing that for me.

Momma said, "Maybe you can talk to James about paying me."

LeAnn said, "That's all right. I will pay you this much." Momma agreed. LeAnn said that she would pay as long as I was getting my education, because she wanted to see me graduate. I hugged her and cried because my sister cared about me and her niece that much. LeAnn told me that she was upset how Mom and Dad would plot to take their kids' money. Remind you, that the state was paying Mom and Dad for me and my child and LeAnn.

LeAnn was going to be 18 soon and they would not get a check for her no more. LeAnn went back to her room and started calculating her money, and then she came out and knocked on Mom and Dad's door. They told her to come in and shut the door behind her. I didn't know what to think. I just went in the room and picked up my baby and held her tight. I just kept thinking that this is too much for my sister. She already has a lot on her, why would Mom put this on her? It's not LeAnn's responsibility to pay for my mistake. Why would they do that to her, why!?

There came a knock on the door and I said come in. It was my little sisters. They asked me could they play with Joyce. I told them yes, so they took her in the other room. They were very careful with her. Joyce really enjoyed her aunts. She was kicking and smiling the whole time that they were playing with her.

With my sisters coming and knocking on the door and getting Joyce to play with took my mind just for a few minutes off the situation. I heard Mom and Dad's door open. LeAnn came in the room. I asked her whether she was okay. She said, "I guess. We worked out a reasonable amount."

I told LeAnn that, "I am so sorry. I will pay you back every penny."

LeAnn said, "Barbara, you are my blood sister and Joyce is my blood niece. I will do anything for y'all."

I said, "Same here. Barbara, I just showed Daddy my check stub and told him that I am already helping you with the bills, Daddy, and Momma's medication, so Dad said that he will get Momma's medication, so I can't pay Momma what she is asking, then Daddy said, 'Ann, she is right,' so they went down on the price, so, Barbara, everything is all right. You can finish school, and Momma will watch Joyce, and I will still have money for savings."

"Thank you, Sis, for doing this for me and your niece." Dottie went in the girls' room and got Joyce and started playing with her till she fell asleep. That gave me time to get her bottles washed and sterilized and time for me to get in a nap also.

The state had sent me mine and Joyce and LeAnn's clothes and shoe vouchers. Joyce was already up and fed, so I decided to try her new clothes on her before she went down for a nap; she looked so cute. I went and showed Mom and the girls. Momma said that she will ask Daddy to take us and LeAnn to Payless for all our shoes. "He might say wait until Saturday since he is off, because school starts up Monday."

Momma told the girls to let her see their shoes and clothes; they did. Momma told me to let Jeanette feed the baby because she wanted to talk to me in her bedroom. She said, "Don't worry about Joyce. The girls know how to feed her, and burp her, and change her diaper."

I said, "Momma, I know they have been helping me with Joyce ever since she was born. I tell them thank you all the time." Then my sisters told Momma that they loved taking care of Joyce.

Momma said, "I know. I have to tell you all not to be in her face so much. Let her breathe." Momma told me to come in the room and shut the door. "I want to talk to you." When Momma said that, I started getting nervous and scared, because you knew with Momma when you were in trouble, because she would have this certain look, but this time she didn't have the look, so I was wondering what was going on. Momma asked me would I mind getting one pair of shoes and let my sisters have the other pairs because they needed shoes badly. She began telling me how Dad had all these bills and I would be doing him a great favor by doing this. I told Momma that I would be glad to help my daddy any way I could. She said, "Thank you, baby." Daddy came home and took us to Payless shoe store and I got one of my sisters a pair of shoes.

The next morning, we got up and dressed for church. This was the first time that Joyce had been to church. She was getting baptized this Sunday, so after she was baptized, Joyce was hungry, so I asked Momma how was I going to warm up her bottle since the church had no water. Momma got Dad's attention and told him the problem. Dad told one of the deacons to turn the water on. He did and I got a pot and warmed up Joyce's milk. I tried to change her, but there was no place to change her. That's when Momma taught me how to change her on my lap.

Momma was a good mother. Even though sometimes she was too hard on us, I thank her for teaching me how to take care of my little girl. Momma said she would talk to Dad about getting me something so I can warm Joyce's milk up and also have something that I can change her on. Everybody in the church wanted to hold her and kiss on her because she was the first baby of the church, but Momma told me to not let everybody kiss on her because she would get germs and, as always, told me to keep her hands washed because she will put them in her mouth, so I did as my mother told me.

That evening, when we got in from church, Momma told me to, "Bathe Joyce and pick out her clothes for a week, and make sure that her milk is made up and all her bottles are washed and sterilized. Before you get yourself ready, make sure she's asleep, because your sisters can't watch her; they have to get ready themselves." Well, Joyce fell asleep and did what Momma told me, maybe not the exact way. I rolled my hair first and picked out my clothes, then I sterilized Joyce's bottles and picked her clothes out for a week for Momma so she didn't have to find Joyce something to wear every day, and I also got her bottles made up and put in the refrigerator like Momma taught me.

Mom and Dad were in the room, watching TV, when Momma called us girls in the room to see what we picked out for school. After Momma saw what we were wearing and she approved, then Daddy called my brother in to see what he was wearing. Erick worked all summer and bought all his school clothes and shoes; he looked real nice. Dad said he was proud of Erick. Dad told Erick to watch over me in high school, and he wanted Erick to make sure that I get to my classes. Erick said, "Yes, sir. I will make sure she gets her schedule and gets to her classes."

The next morning, I kissed my baby bye. She was still asleep, so Mom said, "Don't wake her up." So I just got my school bag and kissed Momma, and my sister and brother and I left. Erick and I walked our sisters to school, because now that Momma was watching the baby, she couldn't walk the girls to school or pick them up; we had to do it. We didn't mind.

We caught our bus across from the school and the bus let us off at the school in the evening to pick our sisters up. The first day of high school was scary for me. Erick showed me where the office was and I got my schedule and looked and saw that I had typing 2. I didn't think I would make it in that class because I barely made in typing 1.

My favorite class was history. I am glad that the day went by fast and that it was almost over with, because I missed my little girl so bad and I kept thinking about, *Is Momma able to take care of my baby by herself, and what if she gets sick? My baby will be all by herself.* I told myself that everything was going to be all right, so finally the bell rang and school was out. Erick came to my class and got me, and we got on the bus together, and we were on our way to my sister's school. We picked them up and headed for home.

When I came in the door, Momma met us and asked how our first day was. We said it was all right. I asked, "Momma, where is Joyce? And did she give you any problem?" She said that Joyce was sleep and she was no trouble at all; Momma said she was a good baby. I was so happy to know that my baby was a good baby. Momma told me that she and Dad had a surprise for me. "Close your eyes. Now open them." I was shocked. She said James bought the baby bed and milk, and diapers, and clothes. He stayed and visited with her, and he was the one that put up the baby's bed. Mom and Dad had bought Joyce a diaper bag, and they bought her a bottle warmer. They had put some more green stamps together and went shopping for their grandchild again.

I was so happy that James had bought his daughter her bed and clothes like he promised. Momma told me that I could call James and talk to him. She said that he was very respectful and he apologized for being disrespectful. After he put the bed up, he played with his little girl and left. I was so happy that James apologized to my mom and to my dad.

After my parents left my room, I started to put all my baby's nice stuff away. Joyce was still asleep in her new baby bed, so that gave me a little time to do my homework before she woke up. I told Dad that they gave me 'Typing 2' this year. He told me that I could use his typewriter anytime. I told Daddy thank you.

Time went and I started to get the hang of being a mother and going to school; my sisters helped me out a lot. School was going pretty good, and Joyce started crawling.

She was getting into everything. She was an explorer. Yes, she was.

On the weekends, the girls would be playing with their dolls or building a house with their toys. I would be either sterilizing bottles, or homework or house chores, then all of a sudden my sisters would be watching Joyce, and as soon as they turned their back, Joyce would be knocking their houses down. The girls would come running to me, telling me that Joyce was destroying their house and could I come and get her. I would come and put Joyce in her bed with her toys and she would play quietly. The girls would move all their toys to my room and watch Joyce till I finished what I was doing.

I came to realize what a big responsibility it was. Trying to go to school and raising a child; it is not easy. I remember when I had Joyce and I had to get up every four hours for those feedings and diaper changes. I thought my life was over, but now Joyce slept through the night and she was eating regular food; what a relief. Joyce was crawling so good that she got into everything and she moved quickly too. Sometimes I would have a lot of homework to do and chores, so I would ask the girls if they could help me with Joyce. They would say yes, but Momma would be in one of her moods and she would tell the girls not to watch Joyce. That would make it so hard on me, I would cry. She would tell the girls that Joyce isn't their responsibility, she is mine, and let me take care of my own baby.

I think when Momma would tell the girls not to help me with Joyce, I think Momma was thinking about me getting pregnant all over again and that was her way of punishing me and taking it out on me; I thought that Momma was being cruel. I never said anything. I just did the best I could by myself.

School was getting better, my typing got better, and my grades were now a C average. LeAnn was able to help me a lot, and also I was happy that I was catching onto what the teachers were teaching me. For the longest time, I thought I was dumb because I wasn't as smart as LeAnn, and that is what I have always been told, that I was dumb, but LeAnn told me that I'm not dumb. It just takes me a while to understand certain things. I still felt that because of all the times that I got chairs cracked over my head and beaten in my head that I was slow, but LeAnn didn't think so. She just kept on saying that I need to try harder.

I said to myself, "What does she know, she can do everything right." She was always in the kitchen, watching Momma cook, not me. I was always doing something else. I really didn't like cooking, so I stayed far away from the kitchen and just took care of my baby.

One day, Daddy came in from work and saw LeAnn getting dinner ready while I was sitting on the living-room floor, playing with Joyce. Daddy said, "Barbara, I don't ever see you in the kitchen, cooking. I always see LeAnn, but not today. What are you getting ready to cook, LeAnn?" LeAnn said meatloaf. Dad told LeAnn to get the baby and watch her. "Barbara, you are going to cook tonight." I was so scared because Daddy was fussing at me and hollering.

Everybody went back to their rooms and I was in the kitchen, so I grabbed a skillet and began putting the hamburger meat all in this skillet, and then LeAnn came out the room and said, "What are you doing, Barbara? That isn't how you fix meatloaf!!!" I was so scared and nervous. I was trying to get the hamburger meat out the skillet before it started cooking and at the same time asking LeAnn to help me. I was in sure panic mode, and LeAnn was laughing so hard at me. She couldn't even help till she got through laughing.

It wasn't funny at all to me. It hurt me to see my blood sister laughing at me. That is how I had been treated in the foster home that beat me. I didn't think that my sister would be one to make fun of me, but she did and it hurt and I will never forget it as long as I live.

I was able to finish dinner with LeAnn teaching me, and the meal came out great, and from that day on, I have stayed in the kitchen, watching and doing, and my cooking had improved a lot. The fear of cooking started leaving me because I learned how to cook, but there were other things that I was scared to try and didn't try because I was scared of failing and I was not so sure of myself. So, fear constantly was a part of me because nobody has ever told me how to get rid of fear.

The school year was moving right along, and before you knew, the school year was over. I was excited but nervous, wondering if I had passed to the 11th grade. I know I did my best, so I hope that my best has paid off. If I failed, Daddy and Momma will be so disappointed in me, and I would be disappointed in me too. I would be letting my whole family down and my little girl down.

My little girl was growing up so fast; she was starting to pull up on things. I knew she would be walking before you knew it. Well, the day came for grade cards. I got mine and I was shocked that I passed to the 11th grade. What excitement! When I saw my brother, Erick, he asked me whether I passed. I showed him my grade card and he showed me his and we both had a big smile on our faces, then we got on the bus and started on our way to our sisters' school; they were standing in the hallway, waiting to show us their grade card. They had also passed; we couldn't hardly wait to show Momma. This was going to be the last year going to school with my brother. I really enjoyed going to school with my brother because he really was a big brother. He constantly looked out for me and I looked out for him also, especially from the girls. My brother had also taken up auto mechanics in school, so he would know how to work on his car that he was going to get this summer.

I was going to miss our pep rallies we would have in school before a big game; they were awesome. They would parade down the hallways with the drums playing and people shouting. The teachers would let us out of our classes for the rest of the day which was only held on Fridays. This was a big thing in Tulsa, Oklahoma, for McClain High School and Booker T. Washington School to play against each other because they were the only African American high schools in Tulsa, OK. And they were rivals, so it was a big event in the black community because everybody either graduated McClain or Booker T.

Time went on and the summer had begun. My little girl was standing up on her own, and it was so funny when she did it because she had this look on her face as to say, "Wow, I'm standing. Are you all watching this? Now what do I do next?" And when I would tell her to come to Momma, she would sit down like to say, "You weren't supposed to see that." I would be laughing so hard, then she would start back crawling away real fast; my little girl was growing up so fast.

James and I were still talking on the phone to one another, and the conversation would get tense sometimes. He would want me to ask Mom and Dad if he could come get his little girl so his family could spend time with her, and James wanted to spend time with me, and I told him that it wasn't possible, that he was going to get me sent away if he pushed the matter. James got mad and hung up. I was so tired of going through this with him and my parents, and to tell you the truth, I was getting over James. I didn't have the same feelings for him that I had, but I knew he was my baby's daddy and we would always have connection, but how can you still have feelings for someone that you never see or spend time with?

Dad came home and we were all in the den, watching TV, and Dad said that he was going to sign us up on the work program in the morning and he told me that I would be signing up too, so know what that means, that I would pay Momma to watch Joyce while I worked. Dad told us to be up and ready by 10:00 a.m. in the morning. I finished watching the program on TV and I went to my room and started getting ready for bed. Joyce was wide awake, so I put her pajamas on and put her in the bed with her toys and she played until she fell asleep, then I fell asleep until LeAnn came in the room and told me that she wanted to talk to me. I asked her what was up.

She said, "Barbara, Mom and Dad are making you go get a job so you can pay her for watching Joyce. I know she doesn't expect me to give her money for Joyce too. I'm not doing that."

I told LeAnn, "Don't worry about it. We will just see if Momma comes to you and me and talks to us, and then we will take it from there, so come on and go to bed."

"Okay, love you, Sis."

"Love you too. Goodnight."

The next morning, Joyce woke me up to be fed and changed, so I just stayed on up. It was about 8:00 a.m. in the morning. I myself dressed and dressed Joyce after she ate, and she was playing and being so loud that she woke up LeAnn, and when LeAnn started talking to her, she just would kick her legs and smile. LeAnn decided that she had to get up too because she had to be at her job at 10:00.

Momma was up in the dining room, having her coffee and reading her bible. She asked me whether Joyce was up. I told her yes, she had already eaten, and she was dressed and, in her bed, playing with her toys. Momma said okay. Then she asked me whether LeAnn was up. And I told her yes.

She called LeAnn in the dining room and told her that she wanted to talk to her after she got off of work. LeAnn said, "Yes, Ma'am." So when we went back in the room, LeAnn said, "Here it comes. What does she want to talk to me about?"

I told LeAnn, "We will find out when you get off of work. I am nervous about working. I hope it isn't going to be a hard job."

"Oh, Barbara, you can do anything you put your mind to, so stop worrying."

Dad was up and dressed. He told me and Erick to come on. He dropped LeAnn at her job and then took us to the place to sign us up. Well, we got signed up, and Erick and I got on at the girl's elementary school. I was so happy that we were working at the same job with the same hours. What a blessing! They told me and Erick that we started Monday and told us who to report to and what we were getting paid an hour. Dad had stayed in the lobby while we did our paperwork, so when I came out, smiling, Dad knew that I had got the job, then he asked Erick whether he got a job. We both told him that we were working together at the girl's school.

"We start Monday at 9:00 a.m. till 4:00 p.m., Monday through Friday."

Dad said, "Oh, that is great, Barbara, and, Erick, you know what, Son? You can work on buying that car you want this summer."

"That's what I'm going to do, Dad."

So when we were getting ready to go home, Dad said that he had to pick up LeAnn from work, so we did. I was so happy to see my sister to tell her the good news of me working. LeAnn got in the car and I told her my good news. She said that she was very happy for me and that she was also happy that I would be working with Erick.

We pulled up to the house and Momma asked, "How did it go?"

I told Momma that, "I am working with Erick at his job that he had last year. We are both going to be working together and we also have the same schedule."

Momma asked, "What will be you all's schedule?" Erick told her 9 a.m. to 4 p.m. Momma told me that after dinner that she wanted to talk to me and Daddy. I said okay. Momma said that she wanted LeAnn to come to the room too. LeAnn looked like 'what is all this about? What does she want now?'

LeAnn said, "Yes, Mamme," and went to her room, and I went to the room too. LeAnn was so upset that she just pasted the floor.

I asked LeAnn, "What do you think Momma wants to talk to you for?"

She said, "Barbara, it's probably about more money."

After a minute or so, Momma and Daddy called us to the room and she told us that they were not going to get any more money from LeAnn when she turned 18 this September. "She will be going off to college anyway, so, Barbara, I am going to charge you the same amount that I was charging your sister, and when you go back to school, I will still keep the baby because D.H.S. is going to pay me for keeping Joyce for you while you are in school. Isn't that a blessing?"

We said, "Yes, Ma'am."

"So everything is worked out, so you all can go and finish doing what you all were doing."

We left the room and went back to our room and LeAnn and I started talking. LeAnn told me that she was so glad that she was turning 18 and going off to college because she was so tired of all the stress that Mom and Dad had taken her through. She said that it was a blessing that I was only paying Momma for the summer to keep Joyce and D.H.S. was paying her while I was in school, so now I could concentrate on my schooling because she wanted me to walk across that stage with my high-school diploma like she did. I told LeAnn that I wanted that more than anything as well and I was going to work real hard to get it.

She said, "Barbara, I know you will."

Saturday came and we all got up and cooked breakfast and started doing our chores. Joyce had been up, playing in her bed, ready for someone to come and get her out of there so she could eat and get into everything. I got her dressed and had her playing while I started the breakfast. Mom and Dad were already up, sitting at the dining-room table, talking, so when Mom heard Joyce, she told me to bring her there. She said that she would put her in the high chair and watch her while I and my sisters cooked breakfast.

Well, we all sat down to breakfast, and when we finished, we cleaned up and then we got started on our chores. We had to, every Saturday, clean the icebox and stove and dust the whole house and vacuum. That had to be done every Saturday, and then once done, Momma would come and check, and if we did it correctly, we could do whatever we wanted to do for the rest of the day. Momma would let us enjoy our time for a minute, then she would call choir rehearsal, because it was church the next day and we had to sing.

My sister, LeAnn, had met this guy named David, and she told Momma about him, and Momma told LeAnn that he was too old for her, but she didn't listen to Momma because she really liked this guy. Momma had talked to Daddy about it, and Daddy told Momma that, "LeAnn will be grown in a couple of months, so let her date that boy if she likes him. LeAnn is very responsible, and look at my and your age difference. LeAnn does not like dating guys her age because she said that they act childish, so she is always going to date older guys, Ann, so don't worry. She is raised right. You are going to have to let her go and make her own decisions, and stop being in these girls' boyfriends' faces. They come to visit them, not you." Momma got mad and slammed the bedroom door.

Well, Erick and I started working all that summer, and I was paying Momma for watching Joyce, and I also was giving Daddy gas money and helping out on some bills. Sometimes Daddy would see my check and he wouldn't take any money. Erick and I didn't work on the weekends, so Erick was able to hang out with his friends and I was able to see James sometimes on the weekends because Momma made sure that I called James.

When Joyce's milk and diapers were getting low, he was always there, taking care of his little girl, but our relationship was going nowhere because of Mom and Dad. They made sure that we weren't ever alone, just there in the front room, playing with our child, with all eyes on us. James would be so mad, and he started complaining that we couldn't be alone with our child or he couldn't take me and Joyce anywhere. I understood what James was talking about because I felt the same way.

He said, "The only way we can see each other is that I sneak on your job to see you. I am tired of sneaking around, Barbara."

"I know, me too, but what can we do about it?" James said that he was going to ask Mom and Dad if he could take me and Joyce to see his mother so she can see her grandchild, so James asked Mom and Dad and they said yes, but I couldn't go, and Momma made it a point to remind James about buying Joyce's milk and diapers.

He said, "She will have milk and diapers when I bring her back."

Even though I couldn't go, I was so happy that James got to take Joyce to see his mother and family. They told James to bring her back in two hours. He said okay and left.

Erick was working at the job, and there was this other janitor working with us. I noticed that he kept staring at me when he was talking to my brother. He was cute. After a while of working with him, he came up to me and asked me did I have a boyfriend. I told him yes, but it didn't matter to him. He was still trying to talk to me. Sometimes James would just pop up at my job to talk with me and my brother. He liked talking to Erick because he said he was easy to talk to, so they became friends, plus Erick didn't agree with how Momma and Dad were keeping James from his child. Erick told me and James that he couldn't wait to graduate and move out. My brother, Erick, always looked out for me and he tried to keep me out of trouble.

One day, while at work, the guy that liked me came over on our lunch break and sat down beside me and starting talking to me, and one thing led to the next and I found myself kissing him, not being aware that James came up there and saw us kissing. I didn't find out that he had come up there to take me to lunch until that Saturday when he came to see Joyce. Jack told me how upset he was by what he had seen, and that was the end of us, but he kept visiting with his child and doing for her.

During the summer, Momma would have us do a general cleaning. She would have us get all our clothes that were too little for us and put them in a bag and give them to some of the kids that were in our neighborhood, which were my sister's size, and give the clothes to them. The parents would tell Momma thank you. Momma was that kind of mother. She was always trying to help somebody.

Erick had saved up enough money to buy his first car. One day, Erick had come to Daddy and asked if he could talk with him and Momma. Daddy took him in the room and told them that he knew what he wanted to do after graduating.

Dad asked, "What is it, Son, that you want to do?"

Erick said, "Join the army." Dad said that it is a good idea. Mom was a little taken back, but Dad told her about all the benefits and opportunities that Erick would have joined the army. After Dad had talked to Mom, she was okay with it, so Dad told Erick after he graduated, he would take him down to the recruiting office. Dad was so proud that Erick wanted to go to the army because Dad had also been in the army, so Dad was extra excited.

It was June now and the summer was starting to heat up. Daddy was on us about the electric bill. He said make sure we cut these lights off and make sure that we cut the TV off at night. We said, "Yes, sir."

One day, we were all in the den and I had Joyce sitting down, playing with her toys, and my sisters started playing with her and they started standing her up, and all of a sudden she started walking. We were so excited that we took her to her grandmother and showed her. After that, Joyce was walking and getting into everything. She was going to turn one in August.

The summer went on and my birthday and Joyce's first birthday had passed, and school was getting ready to start. The first day of school had started, and I was getting my schedule. My classes weren't going to be that hard, so I knew that I could do this.

My brother, Erick, was so busy checking out the girls. When he came across this one girl that caught his eye, he started talking to her and they started going together. She was a senior as well, so they had a lot of classes together. Erick looked at my schedule and told me that he had these classes and he could help me if I needed it. Erick was dating this girl the whole time that he was in school, so one day he asked her if she would want to meet his family.

She said, "Yes. What about this Saturday?"

He said, "Let me see what my family is doing this Saturday, and I will call you." She said okay.

So Erick talked to Mom and Dad and they said that they wanted to meet her too, so that Saturday, Erick drove his car and picked her up, and she came to the house. She was a pretty girl and Erick liked her a lot.

After Erick's girlfriend left, LeAnn and Momma got into it because LeAnn wanted to go with her boyfriend, David, and Momma told her no. LeAnn got mad and moved out and moved with her boyfriend. I was sad that she moved out, but I understood why Momma was too strict, and she couldn't take it no more. I told LeAnn that I would be fine because she was so worried about leaving me. I told her that, "I am going to raise my child and finish school and get out of here too."

Time went on and Joyce and I were doing fine. She was growing up so fast and walking everywhere. She knew at a young age what not to get into because my mother made sure of that. Now it was time to potty-train her, so I asked

James to buy her a potty chair. He couldn't believe that it was that time already.

I had Joyce on a schedule so I could get my schoolwork done, and it worked out perfect. I told Momma not to let her take a nap, and I would put her to bed early so I could do my schoolwork. It worked out great, and Joyce would sleep all night long.

It was already the end of the school year, and now we were getting ready to see my brother graduate. Erick had got his cap and gown and started modeling for the whole family. We were laughing so hard. He looked so nice, but his cap was on backward and he didn't know it. Dad came and put it on him right and told him to make sure when he walked across the stage to make sure that his cap was on straight. Well, it was time for the grade cards to come out and I was feeling real scared, but I knew that I studied real hard this year, but was it enough?

The next day was the day for Erick to graduate, and when we got home, Momma told us to pick out our nice clothes for our brother's graduation, and Momma told me what to let Joyce wear. She was always taking control. I couldn't stand it, but I dared not say nothing, so Dad came home early and dropped Erick at the school and he came back home and got dressed and we all loaded up and headed out to the graduation. While we were in the car, Dad asked when we would get our grade cards.

Renae spoke up and said tomorrow, so Dad said, "Oh boy, I guess I better go to the bank tomorrow and get some money to pass out."

My sisters said, "That's right, Dad."

We got to the graduation and got seated. I decided to take Joyce to the bathroom before the ceremony started. Well, Erick graduated, and after the graduation, Dad took us out for pizza. While we were all eating pizza, Erick told us that when he took Monday to the prom, he asked her to marry him before he went into the service and she said yes. He had bought this girl a ring and everything.

We were shocked but not as shocked as Mom and Dad. They started telling him that he was not ready for marriage. Dad said that they will talk about it later.

Well, we finished the night and we went home and I put Joyce in pajamas because she was out for the count, and then I got myself together and went to bed. It was so nice to have the room all to myself, just me and my little girl.

The next morning, Dad got up and got Erick up and told him to cut the yard and he would take him to the recruiting office when he got off. Mom was sitting at the table, reading her bible, when she told Erick to sit down. She wanted to talk to him. Momma started telling Erick that he wasn't ready for marriage, and then she started bashing his girlfriend, saying that once he went in the service that his girlfriend would forget all about him, so Erick called off the engagement and took his ring back and he went into the service.

Summer was here, and I was so happy because I would be 18 that summer, and my little girl would be going on three years old. Momma and Daddy were still getting a check for me and Joyce. They would keep getting paid until I graduated, so that was a relief for me.

I didn't work that summer because Momma's health started getting worse. I think it was because everybody was leaving home, so I had to keep my little girl just for the summer. Momma said that she would be able to keep Joyce while I was in school. My sisters and I planned on having a great summer. They were older now, so they also helped take care of Momma, and they did the cleaning and cooking as well; we all worked together. My sister, Jeanette, was 14 now, and she had a boyfriend that went to her school named Pete. Jeanette had told Momma and Dad about him, and Dad said that he knew his dad who was a preacher and they also were a gospel group, so Mom and Dad approved of Jeanette dating him. Momma asked Jeanette could Pete sing or play any instruments.

Jeanette said, "Yes, he plays the piano and sings with his family." Momma was so happy that she couldn't wait to meet this boy, so she told Jeanette that she could call him and invite him over. He came over and met the whole family, and then Momma got on the piano and off they went, singing and playing for hours.

My mom enjoyed singing and praising God. The summer was moving so quickly, and the only thing on my mind that I was going to the 12th grade and I would have Mrs. Hopkins as my English teacher. They said that she was tough, but if you did your English notebook right, you could pass her class. I was so lucky that LeAnn and Erick showed me how to do my English notebook, plus LeAnn left hers with me. So I wasn't worried too much because I knew what I was doing just in case she hadn't retired. I was ready; thank God for older sisters and brothers.

One day, after I had got out of school, Mom and Dad said that they needed to talk with me. After I did my homework and gave Joyce her bath and put her down for the night, to come and knock on the door. "Yes, Mamme." Well, I got all my schoolwork done and gave Joyce her bath and fed her, and then she was down for the count, so I went and knocked on my parents' door and they told me to have a seat on the bed and they began talking to me, telling me that the state will be cutting me off when I graduated, then Dad said that I will be grown and it will be time for me to leave the nest. I didn't say anything when Dad said that, but I was thinking to myself that now that Erick and LeAnn were gone and they wouldn't be getting any more money for me and Joyce, that now I had to leave.

Mom and Dad never talked to me about going to college or even encouraged me to maybe go to a trade school. I understood why because they had seen how I struggled in school. I can't blame them for thinking that because I thought it too. I knew that I couldn't make it in college. I wasn't smart like my sister, LeAnn, so I put going to college out of my mind, and how could I go to college with a baby to take care of? Who would keep her? I didn't have anybody but Momma, and she was always getting sick.

School was going great. My senior year, and I got my first-grade card, and I was so proud of myself. I was making good grades in my English class. I made a high C, and in my math class I made a C. The rest were B's.

I couldn't wait to show Mom and Dad, so I hurried up and got on the bus, and when I came home, Momma was playing with Joyce. I only had four classes, so I got out of school at 1:00, so when I came through the door, my little girl just ran to hug her momma and gave me lots of kisses. I put her down with her toys, and Momma was telling me that she was so good and that Joyce never gave her any problems. I told Momma that I was going to change out of my school clothes right quick and that I had something to show her. She said okay, and then she told me that Joyce had fallen asleep on the living-room floor and that I needed to put her in the bed, so I did that and changed my clothes.

When I came out, I told Momma to close her eyes and hold out her hand. I placed my grade card in her hands. When she opened her eyes and saw my grades, she told me how proud she was of me, and then she got up, went to her room, and came back out and told me to shut my eyes and hold out my hand. Then she told me to open my eyes and, to my surprise, it was a brand-new bottle of perfume from her dresser. You see, my mom always had a dresser full of different perfumes; she always smelt good. I was so happy.

She said, "Wait till your daddy gets here. He is going to be so proud that you are doing so well, starting out the 12th grade. I told you that you could do it."

About that time, my sisters came home and showed Momma their grade cards, and she gave them perfume too. Mom told us that we didn't have to cook because she had cooked chili beans and fried chicken and cornbread, so Mom said we could go outside and play kick ball and that she will let me know if Joyce woke up.

Well, Dad came home and he ate, and we showed him our first-grade card. I let my sisters show theirs first; they were so excited, just as I was. Dad looked at their grade cards with a smile on his face, then he reached in his wallet and pulled out the money and gave each of them ten dollars. They hugged Mom and Dad and ran straight two their rooms.

I laughed so hard, then Dad said, "Well, Barbara, let me see yours. I hope that I'm not going to be disappointed." I smiled and gave him my grade card. He hesitated for a minute, then he got up and gave me a big hug and told me that I am starting out the 12 grade on a good note and to keep up the good work. Then he handed me a 20-dollar bill. I hugged them so tight and told them that I am trying my hardest.

My sisters were playing with Joyce and they were having a good time. They loved their niece and she loved them.

Well, I fixed Mom and Dad's plate and brought it to them, and then I fed my daughter and gave her a bath and put her down for the night so I could get my clothes picked out for school and also pick out Joyce's clothes.

I got up that morning for school. Joyce was still asleep. Momma was already up, reading her bible as she always did. I came in to tell her good and that Joyce was still sleeping and that I already got her clothes picked out for the week. She said okay.

My sisters were all dressed and ready to go to school. We kissed Momma goodbye and headed for the bus stop. When I got to school and went to my math class, the teacher stopped me and told me that I didn't do good on my quiz and that I needed to pass this test that was coming up Monday. She said that she would work with me during class hours and that I could make up the test. She asked me whether I had anybody at home that could help me with this worksheet because these were the problems that would be on the test Monday. I said that I might have somebody that can help me. So while I was in class, the teacher took time out to help me. I kept remembering what Mom said. She would tell me that I can do all things through Christ who strengthens me. So while I was in class, I started understanding how to work these fractions, and my teacher said that I was getting the hang of it.

The bell rang, and as I was going out the door, my teacher told me to get somebody to help me. My next class was English. Mrs. Hopkins told everybody that she wanted to see how we were coming along with our English notebooks and to make sure we had everything in our notebooks that we needed, so she checked students' notebooks. Some students hadn't even started on theirs. When she came to me, she told me good job. I was so happy that she told me that. It made me feel better about what I had to learn.

School was over for the day, and I was wondering when I'd tell Momma about me needing help with my math and if I called LeAnn to help me, would she say yes. Because Momma was angry at LeAnn for moving out and moving in with her boyfriend, Momma said that LeAnn was committing sin, living with her boyfriend and not being married.

I got home. Momma was feeding Joyce her lunch. I hugged my little girl and kissed Momma and told her I wanted to talk to her about something. She said, "Okay, let me get Joyce cleaned up and I will get her toys for her to play with and we can talk."

We got Joyce settled down with her toys and me and Momma talked. I told her what the teacher said and then I asked her if I could call LeAnn over to help me.

Mother told me that I could call LeAnn, "But, Barbara, she might be at work, but try her anyway," so I did, and my sister answered. I was happy to hear her voice and she was so happy to hear from me. She asked me how everybody was doing. I told her that everybody was fine, and then she asked me about her niece. I told her that she was getting so big. She began to tell me with a trembling voice how much she missed me and her niece.

I asked her, "How would you like to see us today?"

She said, "Baby girl, I would love to see you and my niece, but how?" I told her that I was struggling in math and my teacher asked whether I had anybody to help me.

"I told her that I had you, so I came home and asked Momma could I call you over to help me, and she said yes." I could tell that LeAnn had a smile on her face. "So, will you come?"

She said, "I'm on my way."

I said, "Great. We will be waiting."

So when she showed up, Momma gave her a big hug. LeAnn was shocked that Momma greeted her like that. Momma told her to come in and have a seat while I went and got Joyce. When Joyce saw her aunt, she went right to her and kissed her aunt, and LeAnn started crying and Joyce wiped her tears and got down and started playing with her toys. LeAnn told me that we better get started because she could only stay for an hour because she had to go home and cook, so we got started.

First, I didn't understand what she was teaching me, but LeAnn kept going over it and I finally got the hang of it. I was so happy that I finally now knew how to do the math. LeAnn was so happy that she was able to help me. She told me that I was not slow; it just took me a little while to catch on, but once I got it, I didn't forget. That made me feel good.

She asked me did I have Mrs. Hopkins. I told her yes. LeAnn taught me how to study and how to fix my English notebook for Mrs. Hopkins so I could pass. LeAnn had about 30 minutes before she had to go. She took those minutes and she and Momma talked. Momma said that she wanted LeAnn to come over more often. LeAnn said that she would. She hugged us and then she left. Momma and I were so happy to see Joyce. Momma was really happy, so happy, that she started shouting and thanking God for letting her see LeAnn. Momma acted tough, but she still had a soft spot for her children.

When I came in the room to see what Joyce was doing, she had fallen asleep on the floor with her toys; it was so cute. I put her in the bed and tucked her in with her doll. About that time, the girls were coming in from school, and Mom had told them that they just missed their sister. They were sad about not seeing her, but Momma told them that LeAnn told her that she would try to come and see them this Saturday. They were glad about that. They asked where Joyce was. I said taking a nap, so the girls went in their rooms. Meanwhile, I was working on my math problems, trying to finish before Joyce woke up. It was easy now that I knew how to do it.

I was ready for that makeup test tomorrow and ready for the test on Monday. I had so much confidence now, more than I have ever had. I went to school and took my makeup test and passed.

I got home and was working on my English notebook. I worked night and day because I was determined to graduate. My grades were improving, and Dad was getting broke. He said that he will be glad when I graduate so he won't have to give me any more money; we laughed.

Senior year was always very costly. They started sending out notices to parents about senior's cap and gown and pictures.

When Mom showed Dad, he said, "Where did the year go?" And then he told me that he didn't have the money to buy my senior pictures when I'd take them next week. "Maybe if you check with your sister, she might be able to buy them."

After I left Mom and Dad, I went to the kitchen to call LeAnn, to ask if she could buy my senior pictures. She answered the phone and I asked her if she could buy my senior pictures. She asked when I was taking the pictures. I told her, "Next Monday, and I have to have the money too." She said that she could buy them and fix my hair and that she had a dress that I could borrow that would look beautiful on me. She said that she would come to the house next Sunday to do my hair and she would bring me the dress over as well. LeAnn told me not to worry, that I would have my senior pictures.

That week went by and LeAnn came over to do my hair. We all were happy to see her. She visited with Mom and Dad and it was a good visit. Dad told her, "Thank you for buying Barbara's pictures." She said that she was happy to do it.

Well, she did my hair and I tried on the dress and it fit perfect. I modeled for the whole family and they told me that I was so pretty. I started blushing. LeAnn gave me the money and then she started playing with her niece for a while, and then she had to leave.

Monday, I got up early for school so I could pick Joyce's clothes out for Momma so she wouldn't have to do it. Momma was up, making sure that my sisters looked nice going to school, then she asked me to get Joyce's barrettes out, that she was going to do Joyce's hair, so I did, and then I kissed her goodbye and went to school.

I enjoyed my senior year because I was doing so well in school. We took our senior pictures. I paid for mine and went back to my English class. Mrs. Hopkins had us turn in our English notebooks. She said that she would be grading them this Thursday and she would return them to us on Friday. She reminded us that the English notebook was 85% of our grade, and if we were doing poorly in my class, that the English notebook could pull our grade up to passing. The pictures came in that Thursday. I couldn't wait to open them. I did and they were beautiful. I couldn't wait to show the family and my sister.

The day was over, and when I came through the door, my little girl ran to me and jumped in my arms. Momma had done her hair and had her dressed; she was so pretty. I told Momma thank you and kissed her. She said that Joyce did very well getting her hair done. I showed Momma the pictures. She said that I was beautiful and then she told me that she wanted a big picture. I told her that I had to let LeAnn pick what size she wanted and then I would give her one. She said, "That's right, because LeAnn is the one who paid for them, so that's only fair."

Momma had cooked her famous spaghetti and big meatballs. She had the whole house smelling so good. Well, I called LeAnn to tell her my pictures and cap and gown came in and she needed to come and get her picture, and then I said, "Thank you again for buying my senior pictures."

She said, "You are welcome." LeAnn said that she would come over when the girls got out school because she wanted to see them and her niece. I told her that it would be fine because Joyce would be up from her nap about then, "And you know she is going to want to see her aunt."

The girls came in from school and I showed them my senior pictures. They said that they were beautiful, then my sister, Jeanette, said that she couldn't wait for her picture to be put on the piano with ours. I told Jeanette that it won't be long and it will be up there with ours. She smiled and asked me could she have a wallet-size picture to carry in her purse. I said yes and gave her and my other sisters one. About that time, Renae told me that Joyce was up. Renae went into the room and picked Joyce up and brought her into the living room. I told Renae to put that big girl down. "She can walk; she is not a baby no more." I showed Joyce my picture and asked her who that was, and she said in a flash, "Momma."

As soon as she said that, a knock came at the door and it was LeAnn. Joyce ran right to her, and all her sisters hugged her, then Momma came out and hugged LeAnn and asked her whether she wanted some coffee. LeAnn said yes. Momma told me to put on some coffee.

I said, "Yes, Ma'am," and then Mom and LeAnn sat down at the table. When she sat down, she saw my pictures and tears began to run down her face. She said how beautiful I looked and that she was so proud of me.

Momma hugged her and said, "You should be proud." Then Mom asked if she could get her picture now so she can put me up there on the piano with LeAnn. She got the picture and put my picture on the piano alongside my sister. LeAnn said that she and I looked so much alike.

Momma got on the piano and we started singing. We were having a good time, and then we heard Dad pull up, and when he saw LeAnn, he was happy to see her, and he started telling her how Momma talked about her all the time. "We really miss you."

Well, LeAnn stayed for about two hours and then she left. I showed Daddy my picture and he smiled and said that it was a beautiful picture. Dad told Mom and me that LeAnn didn't seem happy, "And it seemed like she didn't want to leave. Did you all get that same feeling?"

I told Dad that I did; something was going on with my sister, but I didn't know what. She didn't look that happy. LeAnn was always rushing home to cook. We told her how the family and I enjoyed her, and I thanked her again for buying my pictures.

She said, "No problem, baby girl. I am going now to buy a frame and put it in the living room of my house." Then she called for her niece and sisters to tell them that she was leaving. Joyce started crying, saying that she wanted to go with her aunt. LeAnn told her that she would come and get her Saturday. I showed Daddy my cap and gown, and he asked me when the graduation was. I told him in two weeks, then he asked me whether I was going to the prom this Friday. I told him no, that nobody had asked me, "So I will be here with my sisters, watching movies and eating popcorn with my sisters, and if LeAnn can't keep Joyce, I will be here, taking care of my little girl."

As Daddy was walking away, he made a comment, saying, "Yeah, you miss out on a lot when you have a child and have such a great responsibility," and then he walked off and went to his room. I put my head down and walked to my bedroom.

Monday came and I went to school, and it was time for cap and gown rehearsal, and time for grade cards to come out that Wednesday. I was so stressed that week, hoping that I had passed.

When school let out and I came home, I checked my notebook and made sure everything was in order. I felt good about the rest of my classes because all my test scores were passing.

Wednesday came. I got up, feeling very anxious. As I got my things together, I went in the kitchen, and Momma was at the table, reading her bible. We didn't like to disturb Momma while she was reading, but I just had to interrupt her this day. Momma looked up from her bible and asked me what I wanted. I told Momma that the day was grade-card day and that I wanted her to pray that I had passed. She said that she was already praying for all her kids in school, that the only thing I needed to do was believe and claim it.

I said, "Yes, Ma'am," and kissed her goodbye, and she told me to have a good day. I kept thinking about what Momma said, so when I got to class, I felt better, so when Mrs. Hopkins passed out the grade cards and our English notebooks, she looked at me and smiled, so when I opened my grade card, I was shocked. I made a B in her class and a B on my English notebook. I was so excited that the tears began to roll down my face. I composed myself. Mrs. Hopkins said that she was proud of her class because we worked real hard, and since we were at the end of the school year, we could be dismissed and go to our other classes.

When I got to my other classes, I had got my grade card and I passed all my classes. *I am going to graduate. Wait till I tell Mom and Dad and my sister, LeAnn.* I was on cloud ten all day. We had to go to our classes, but we didn't do anything but have parties and watch movies the rest of the week.

I had to stay after school for graduation rehearsal, so Dad was going to pick me up. I couldn't wait to show him my report card. The rehearsal went well. I got my things together, and as I was leaving the building, I saw that Dad was already there waiting on me. I got in the car and I asked him had he been waiting for a long time. He said no, that he had just been sitting for a few minutes, so he decided to read his word till I came out.

He asked me, "How was rehearsal?"

I told him, "Good. I just hope that I can remember which hand to shake with and which hand to grab the diploma with." Dad laughed and said that I will do fine. "Thanks, Dad. Oh yeah, I forget. I have a surprise for you." Then I pulled out my grade card.

He was so happy for me, then he said, "Barbara, I told you. If you worked hard and applied yourself, you would bring home good grades, and I know that you were working hard and praying."

"Dad, I was working real hard. I can't wait to show Mom. She has been praying for me also." I told Dad that the graduation was Friday at 7:00 p.m. "I have to be here at the school at 6:00. We are having it in the gymnasium." Dad told me that he already told at his work that he had to leave early Friday because his daughter that he was proud of was graduating.

Dad and I had a good time talking as we rode home, and when we pulled up in the driveway, Momma and Joyce were sitting on the porch, enjoying a nice day. Joyce was riding her little toy that her dad brought her. I went up to Mom and kissed her on the cheek, and Joyce came running too and gave me and her papa a big hug. After that, she went back to riding her toy. After that, I handed Momma my grade card and she started crying. She told me that she knew I could do it with god's help. Then she told me that God had already told her that I passed. I smiled at her, then she told me that she had a surprise for me. "Barbara, I cooked you your favorite dish, tuna casserole."

Then about that time, my sisters came home and showed Mom and Dad their grade cards, and they had passed also. Daddy started reaching in his back pocket. He pulled out his wallet and started passing out money. We all had a smile on our faces. I asked Mom if I could call LeAnn to tell her that I passed. She said yes. The girls said that they were going to put their books up and go back and play with Joyce. "So you can talk to LeAnn and tell her that we passed too."

I said, "I will make sure that I tell her."

When I dialed my sister's number, she picked up and I told her the good news and I told her that her other sisters also passed.

She said, "Tell them good job." She asked me whether I knew how many people were coming to my graduation.

I said, "No, but I sent everybody I know an invitation." I knew that my aunts and uncles were going to be there because they told me. My family for sure was going to be there and that was all that mattered. Friday came, and Mom and Dad were getting ready, and the girls were also. I got my little girl and myself dressed, and then I waited for Dad to take me to the school.

When Mom and Dad came out the room, they looked and smelled so nice. Dad went on and took me to the school, and he said that they would be up there as soon as LeAnn came to the house. I said okay, then he said again how proud of me he was and that I looked real nice in my cap and gown. Then he drove off and I went into the gym.

It was time for us to line up for the ceremony. I was nervous and happy all at the same time. I kept thinking, *Lord, don't let me trip or shake with the wrong hand or drop my diploma.* All this was running through my head. The ceremony started. I saw my little girl walk in with my family; she looked so beautiful. When they called my name, my family started yelling my name and I heard my sister yell that she loved me. I walked across that stage with my head held high. I was so proud of myself, and I knew my baby girl was proud of her mother.

After the graduation was over, Dad took us out for pizza. I received that diploma in May of 1983. What a year.

The End

www.ingramcontent.com/pod-product-compliance
Lightning Source LLC
Chambersburg PA
CBHW070654250726
48662CB00001B/122